John's Gospel

by Rex Jackson

*Developed in Cooperation with
the ICI International Office Staff*

INTERNATIONAL CORRESPONDENCE INSTITUTE
P.O. Box 50848
Fort Worth, Texas 76105
USA

John's Gospel

Address of the ICI office in your area:

Scripture quotations are from the New International Version (NIV) and Good New Bible (Today's English Version).
© American Bible Society, 1976. Used by permission. The King James's Version (KJV) is also quoted.

To be used with: Student Report 1991 Edition

First Edition 1969
Second Edition 1978
Third Edition 1980
Fourth Edition 1984
Fifth Edition 1986
　　Reprinted 1987
Sixth Edition 1991

© 1969, 1978, 1980, 1984, 1986, 1991
All Rights Reserved
International Correspondence Institute
Irving, Texas, USA
6/91 5M BA

L2320E93   ISBN 1-56390-017-3

Contents

		Page
	First, Let's Have a Talk.............................	5

Lesson		
1	John 1	10
2	John 2	28
3	John 3	34
4	John 4	42
5	John 5	48
6	John 6	54
7	John 7	64
8	John 8	74
9	John 9	82
10	John 10	88
11	John 11	94
12	John 12	104
13	John 13	114
14	John 14	122
15	John 15	130
16	John 16	138
17	John 17	146
18	John 18	156
19	John 19	166
20	John 20	174
21	John 21	182

First, Let's Have a Talk

A Word from Your Study Guide Author

This course is about a person who was born almost 2,000 years ago. Why should you study it? How can it affect your life? How can these lessons help you? Whatever your religion may be, you owe it to yourself to know something about Jesus - His life, His teachings and His claims.

Are you looking for a source of new power and happiness in your life? You can find it in these lessons. The Good News written so long ago has the best solutions available for twentieth century problems. Do you want to find reality in your spiritual life? Or strengthen your faith? Or know God better?

You will find what you are looking for as you follow the instructions in this study guide. A modern method of teaching yourself helps you to learn the principles easily and put them into practice immediately.

Your Study Guide

John's Gospel is a pocket-sized workbook that you can take with you and study whenever you have some free time. Try to set aside some time every day to study it. If you are studying this course with a group, follow the instructions of your group leader.

How to Answer Study Questions

There are different kinds of study questions in this study guide. Below are samples of several types and how to answer them.

A MULTIPLE-CHOICE question or item asks you to choose an answer from the ones that are given.

Example of Multiple-Choice Question

1 A week has a total of
a) 10 days.
b) 7 days.
c) 5 days.

The correct answer is *b) 7 days*. In your study guide, make a circle around *b)* as shown here:

1 A week has a total of
a) 10 days.
b) 7 days.
c) 5 days.

(For some multiple-choice items, more than one answer may be correct. In that case, you would circle the letter in front of each correct answer.)

First, Let's Have a Talk 7

A *TRUE-FALSE* question or item asks you to choose which of several statements are TRUE.

Example of True-False Question

2 Which statements below are TRUE?
  a) The Bible has a total of 120 books.
  ⓑ) The Bible is a message for believers today.
  c) All of the Bible authors wrote in the Hebrew language.
  ⓓ) The Holy Spirit inspired the writers of the Bible.

Statements **b** and **d** are true. You would make a circle around these two letters to show your choices, as you see above.

A *MATCHING* question or item asks you to match things that go together, such as names with descriptions, or Bible books with their authors.

Example of Matching Question

1 Write the number for the leader's name in front of each phrase that describes something he did.

..**1**..a Received the Law at Mount Sinai   1) Moses
..**2**..b Led the Israelites across Jordan   2) Joshua
..**2**..c Marched around Jericho
..**1**..d Lived in Pharaoh's court

Phrases **a** and **d** refer to *Moses*, and phrases **b** and **c** refer to *Joshua*. You would write **1** beside **a** and **d**, and **2** beside **b** and **c**, as you see above.

Your Student Report

If you are studying to earn a certificate or a seal, you have received a separate booklet called *Student Report Question Booklet, John's Gospel*. There are two sections in this booklet with removable answer sheets in the center of the booklet. Your study guide will tell you when to complete each section.

Follow the instructions given in your student report for sending the answer sheets to the ICI office in your area. The address should be stamped in the front of this study guide or on the back of the student report question booklet. If it is not there, send the answer sheets to the ICI Brussels address given on the back of the student report question booklet. When you do this, you will receive an attractive certificate. Or if you have already earned the certificate by completing another course in this unit of courses, you will receive a seal.

About the Author

Rex Jackson is an instructor of journalism at Evangel College, Springfield, Missouri. Mr. Jackson, an ordained minister of the Assemblies of God, was a missionary to Nigeria for 25 years, and taught for three years at West Africa Advanced School of Theology in Togo, West Africa. He served as acting president of the school for two years. During that time he wrote or developed various kinds of church literature, such as training books, Sunday School literature, and correspondence courses.

Mr. Jackson holds a Bachelor of Arts degree in Bible from Central Bible College, Springfield,

Missouri, and a Master of Science degree in journalism from Kansas State University, Manhattan, Kansas.

Lesson 1: John 1

In this lesson you will study...

Good News by a Man Named John
John Learns the Good News
John Shares the Good News
The Word of Life
The Eternal Word
Light and Life
The Word Becomes a Man
John the Baptist's Message
The Lamb of God
The First Disciples of Jesus
Jesus Calls Philip and Nathanael

GOOD NEWS BY A MAN NAMED JOHN

Objective 1. *Identify the author of John's Gospel.*

John Learns the Good News

Almost 2,000 years ago a young fisherman named John left his boats and nets in order to follow a teacher called Jesus. For three and a half years he and eleven other men went with Jesus from town to town in the country of Palestine. They were His disciples or students.

John and the other disciples learned very well the lessons Jesus taught about God and His love for all people. John knew Jesus very well. He was His closest friend.

John and the other disciples learned from Jesus the good news that we call the gospel. Gospel means good news. They learned that Jesus was the Son of God. Jesus had come to earth to save men, women, boys, and girls from their sins and to give them eternal life. Before Jesus went back to heaven He told the disciples to share this good news with everyone on earth.

Jesus promised the disciples that the Holy Spirit would help them remember all the things that He had taught them. The Holy Spirit would help them share the good news with others.

For You To Do

In the following exercises, circle the letter in front of the correct answer.

1. Who was John, the follower of Jesus?
   a) John the Baptist
   b) A fisherman who became Jesus' closest friend
   c) A carpenter from Galilee

2. How long did John stay with Jesus and hear His teaching?
   a) Three and a half weeks
   b) Three and a half months
   c) Three and a half years

3. What does *gospel* mean?
   a) Good news
   b) Message about God
   c) Life of Christ

Check your answers with those at the end of this lesson.

John Shares the Good News

John spent his whole life telling people the good news that he had learned from Jesus. When he was an old man, God told him to write the good news. Copies would be made of it for people all over the world. God wanted John to share the good news with us as well as with the people who lived then.

God let John know just exactly what he should write. The Holy Spirit brought to his memory the very words that Jesus had said. He wrote down the important truths that Jesus had taught him so carefully. John recorded these truths in the New Testament book that is called by his name. We know it as the Gospel of John.

In the same way, the Holy Spirit inspired John to write four other books. Three of them were letters. One was a revelation of what would happen in the future. We have these five books, along with other inspired writings, in the Bible.

John wrote his book in a language that the people would understand: Greek. Since we do not understand Greek, the Bible has been translated into our language: English. There are many translations of the Bible into English. The one which is suggested for the study of this course is the *Good News Bible*, also known as *Today's English Bible*.

For You To Do

Circle the letter in front of the correct answer.

4 Where did John learn the good news that he was to share with everyone?
 a) From Jesus
 b) From the newspapers
 c) From his parents

5 When did John write his book about the life of Jesus?
   a) When he was a young man traveling with Jesus.
   b) When he was an old man, after he had taught many people about Jesus.
   c) When he was a fisherman, before he knew Jesus.

6 How did John know what to write in his five books that we have in the New Testament?
   a) The Holy Spirit of God put in his mind what he was to write.
   b) He was inspired by reading other books about Jesus.
   c) A committee planned it.

Check your answers.

THE WORD OF LIFE

Objective 2. *Identify the Word of Life.*

Read John 1:1-18.

If you are using a *Good News Bible*, the title used for chapter 1, verses 1 through 18 of the Gospel of John, is "The Word of Life."

These verses are very important because they tell us who Jesus really is and why He came to this earth. They are the introduction that John wrote for his book.

John 1

All the rest of John's gospel explains the truths that we have in these first verses.

The Eternal Word

Read John 1:1-3 again.

We let people know what we think by our words. God has let us know what He thinks in two ways: through His written Word, the Bible, and through His Son Jesus who came to earth to tell us about God. Jesus is God's living Word. In all these verses John is writing about Jesus, the living Word. Verse 14 says that the Word became a human being. Jesus is called the Word because God speaks to us through Him.

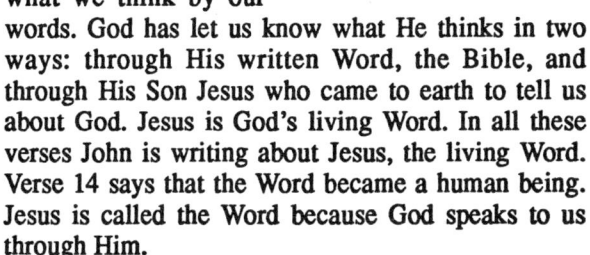

> God...in these last days...has spoken to us through his Son (Hebrews 1:1-2).

From John 1:1-3 we learn that Jesus was with God from the beginning. Jesus is God. This does not mean that there are two Gods. There is only one God but He is a trinity—three persons in one. God is Father, Son, and Holy Spirit. Each of the three has a special work to do. They have always worked together.

God the Father, Jesus the Son, and the Holy Spirit have always been. They are eternal, without beginning or ending. Jesus was born on earth and is called the Son of God, but He had always lived in heaven before that.

Verse 3 says that all things were made by Him, that is by Jesus. We read about this in another part of the Bible.

For through him God created everything in heaven and on earth (Colossians 1:16).

Jesus Christ gave life to all things we see in the world. Also, Jesus gives eternal life to those who repent of their sins and believe in Him as their personal Savior.

Whoever has the Son has this life; whoever does not have the Son of God does not have life (1 John 5:12).

For You To Do

Circle the letter in front of the correct answer.

7 Jesus is called "the Word" because
a) God speaks to us through Him.
b) He preached the gospel.
c) we read about Him in a book.

8 When did Jesus' life begin?
a) When He was born as a baby in Bethlehem.
b) His life never had a beginning; He is eternal.
c) He was created by God when God created the earth.

9 What kind of life does Jesus give?
   a) He gives life only to things in the world; all things were created by Him.
   b) He gives eternal life only to those who trust in Him.
   c) He gives both natural life and eternal life; He made the world and saves those who believe in Him.

Check your answers.

Light and Life

Read John 1:4-13 again.

Verse 4 tells us that the life of Jesus brought light to men. Just as the light lets us see where to walk, Jesus shows us how to live. He shows us the way to heaven.

Many people do not want to accept Jesus. They would rather walk in the darkness of their own ways. But those who do receive Jesus as their personal Savior are given the right to become God's children.

Although we were created by God, this did not make us His children. We have all done wrong and are sinners by nature. Our sins separate us from God. But when we accept Jesus as our Savior, He takes away our sin and gives us a new nature. He changes us so that we will not keep on doing wrong. We call this great change our new birth. Through it God becomes our Father and we become His children.

We become the children of God, not through anything that we do for ourselves but through being born of God. We are not the sons of God by natural birth. You might say, "I was born a Christian. My father and mother were Christians." Your parents being Christians does not make you a Christian. You are a Christian only when you are born of God.

For You To Do

Circle the letter in front of the correct answer.

10 Jesus is called "the Light" because
   a) He carried a lamp to show us where to walk on the path.
   b) He teaches us how to live and shows us the way to heaven.

11 Who have the right to be called the children of God?
   a) Only those who receive Jesus as their personal Savior.
   b) All men because all men are created by God.

12 How do we become children of God?
   a) By being born of Christian parents who are serving God.
   b) By being born in a Christian nation where there are many churches.
   c) By being born of God when we receive Jesus as our Savior.

Check your answers.

John 1

The Word Becomes a Man

Read John 1:14-18 again.

This is the greatest thing that happened in the history of the world: God became a man. He loved us so much that He came to take our punishment, to die for our sins.

But as God, Jesus could not die. He had to have a human body in order to die for us. So Jesus was born as a baby in Bethlehem. The Son of God became a man so that He could make men the sons of God.

God gave the law through Moses to let us know what He wants us to do. We could not keep the laws of God. They let us see that we needed a Savior. That Savior is Jesus. In Him we receive God's grace: God's pardon for our sins and a wonderful new life full of blessing as His children.

For You To Do

Circle the letter in front of the correct answer.

13 Why did Jesus become a man?
  a) So that He could die to save us from our sins.
  b) So that He could teach us.
  c) So that He could know us.

JOHN THE BAPTIST'S MESSAGE

Objective 3. *Explain the message of John the Baptist.*

Read John 1:19-28.

Read again verses 6 through 10 and verse 15. These verses all tell us about John the Baptist, God's messenger. This is not the John who was a disciple of Jesus.

Great crowds went to hear John preach. Some people thought that he might be the Messiah or Christ, the Savior that God had promised to send. John let them know that he was only God's messenger, sent to tell them to get ready to receive the Messiah. He told them to repent and turn away from sin. When they did, he baptized them.

When a great king traveled in Bible times, he sent a messenger ahead of him to let all the people know that he was coming. This is what John did for Jesus.

For You To Do

Circle the letter in front of the correct answer.

14 What did John the Baptist do?
  a) He wrote the Good News.
  b) He told the people that the Messiah was coming.
  c) He said He was the Messiah.

THE LAMB OF GOD

Objective 4. *Explain why Jesus is called The Lamb of God.*

Read John 1:29-34.

John the Baptist had known Jesus since they were small boys. Their mothers were cousins. Yet John did not know who Jesus really was until God revealed it to him. God showed John that Jesus was the Messiah: the sacrifice for sinners, the one who would baptize with the Holy Spirit, the Son of God.

Many people, as did John, think of Jesus as just a good man. We all need to meet Him personally and know Him better. These lessons will help you know Jesus better.

Jesus was called the Lamb of God because lambs were a sacrifice for sin. Those who had sinned and deserved to die could ask God to accept the death of a lamb in their place. Jesus is the Lamb that God sent to die in our place to take away our sin.

For You To Do

Circle the letter in front of the correct answer.

15 In what way was Jesus the Lamb of God?
   a) He was as gentle as a lamb.
   b) He was a sacrifice for sin.

THE FIRST DISCIPLES OF JESUS

Read John 1:35-42.

Two of those who were disciples (followers) of John went with Jesus. One was Andrew; the other is not named. He may have been John, the writer of the gospel you are studying.

Andrew went to get his brother Simon who is called Peter also. Andrew said that he believed Jesus was the Messiah. Messiah means "Christ" or the "Anointed One."

For You To Do

Circle the letter in front of the correct answer.

16 Name Jesus' first disciples.
  a) Matthew, Mark, Luke, John
  b) Mary, Joseph, Nathanael
  c) Andrew, Peter, and probably John

JESUS CALLS PHILIP AND NATHANAEL

Objective 5. *Explain why Nathanael and Philip decided to follow Jesus.*

Read John 1:43-51.

Philip is a good example for us. He told Nathanael about Jesus. At first Nathanael would not believe that Jesus was the Messiah. Some people do not believe at first what we tell them about Jesus. Philip said, "Come and see."

When Nathanael went to see for himself, he was convinced that Jesus was the Son of God. Anyone who goes to Jesus in prayer with a sincere heart can know the truth about who Jesus is. Jesus will reveal Himself.

In verse 51 Jesus calls Himself the Son of Man. This name is used thirteen times in John's gospel. It reminds us that the Son of God left His throne in heaven and became a man. He had a body just like ours. He understands our problems. He too was tempted but He did not sin. He always did the will of God. As Son of Man, Jesus showed us what perfect manhood can be by the help of God. And as Son of Man He represented all mankind before God. He died as a substitute for all mankind.

John begins his Good News by telling us who Jesus is. In this first chapter he presents these names of Jesus; the Word, Jesus, Lamb of God, Messiah, Christ, Teacher, Son of God, King of Israel, and Son of Man.

For You To Do

17 In the first chapter of the Gospel of John, several different names are used for Jesus. See how many you can find.

18 Find the verse that you like best in this chapter and memorize it.

19 Thank Jesus for coming to die for your sins. Ask Him to speak to you and let you know Him better.

20 Pray for all the other persons who are studying this course that they may know Jesus better.

John 1

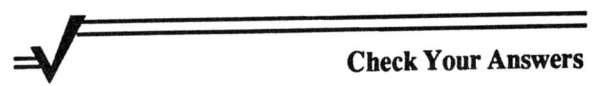

Check Your Answers

The answers to your study exercises are not given in the usual order, so that you will not see the answer to your next question ahead of time. Look for the number you need, and try not to look ahead.

9 c) He gives both natural life and eternal life; He made the world and saves those who believe in Him.

1 b) A fisherman who became Jesus' closest friend.

10 b) He teaches us how to live and shows us the way to heaven.

2 c) Three and a half years.

11 a) Only those who receive Jesus as their personal Savior.

3 a) Good news.

12 c) By being born of God when we receive Jesus as our Savior.

4 a) From Jesus.

13 a) So that He could die to save us from our sins.

5 b) When he was an old man, after he had taught many people about Jesus.

14 b) He told the people that the Messiah was coming.

6 a) The Holy Spirit of God put in his mind what he was to write.

15 b) He was a sacrifice for sin.

7 a) God speaks to us through Him.

16 c) Andrew, Peter, and probably John.

8 b) His life never had a beginning; He is eternal.

Lesson 2: John 2

In this lesson you will study...
The Wedding at Cana
Jesus Goes to the Temple
Jesus Knows All Men

THE WEDDING AT CANA

Objective 1. *Explain the significance of Jesus' first miracle at the marriage feast at Cana.*

Read John 2:1-12.

Jesus, His mother, and His disciples went to a wedding. According to the custom, wine was served at the feast. Before the feast was over, the wine was all gone.

Jesus was always ready to help people. Mary, His mother, asked Him to do something so that the couple would not be embarrassed at their wedding. It would take the power of God, a miracle, to meet this need. Mary had no right to tell Jesus to do a miracle. Only God, His Father, had that right.

Jesus was not sure that it was time for Him to start doing miracles, but God must have let Him know that it was. He turned water into wine and met the need. The Son of God can do anything.

For You To Do

1 What were the results of Jesus' first miracle?
  a) Mary realized her place of importance.
  b) He demonstrated His glory and His disciples believed on Him.
  c) Jesus became good friends with the bridegroom.

JESUS GOES TO THE TEMPLE

Objective 2. *Explain the spiritual lesson of Jesus cleansing the Temple.*

Read John 2:13-22.

Every year the people of God went to His house in Jerusalem to celebrate the Passover. They sacrificed lambs in memory of the Passover lamb that had saved their people from death long ago. When the angel of death was going to pass through the land, God had told His people what to do. Each family had killed a lamb and put its blood on the door. The death angel passed over every house marked by the blood of a lamb. In all the other houses the oldest son died.

All this was a picture of how Jesus, the Lamb of God, was going to save people

John 2

from eternal death. And the Passover celebration was a very important kind of worship to God.

Everyone should have been very respectful and worshipful in God's house. Instead of that, some traders were ruining everything. Jesus drove them out because they were just making a business out of religion.

Jesus refused to do a miracle just to show people who He was. He did all of His miracles to help people. But He did mention the greatest miracle of all which would prove that He was the Son of God. He spoke of His body as the house of God because God lived in Him. The people would destroy it, kill His body later on right there in Jerusalem, but in three days He would rise again from the grave. However, the people did not understand what He meant.

For You To Do

2 What did Jesus do in the temple at Jerusalem?
 a) He drove the traders and money-changers away.
 b) He made a sacrifice.
 c) He tore the temple down and rebuilt it.

3 What lesson did Jesus teach while in the temple?
 a) That the temple was the place to do business.
 b) That He would destroy that very temple and build it again in three days.
 c) That His body was a temple. He would die and arise from the grave after three days.

JESUS KNOWS ALL MEN

Read John 2:23-25.

One reason we are studying this course is so that we can understand who Jesus really is and what He can do for us. In Jerusalem many persons believed in Jesus when they saw the miracles that He did. Let us believe what the Bible teaches about Jesus.

Many people say they believe in Jesus but do not act like it. If we believe that Jesus is the Word, we will believe what He taught. If we believe that His life is our light, we will follow where He leads. If we believe that He is the Lamb of God, we will accept Him as the sacrifice for our sins.

For You To Do

4 Memorize John 2:25.

John 2

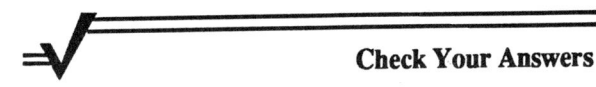

Check Your Answers

The answers to your study exercises are not given in the usual order, so that you will not see the answer to your next question ahead of time. Look for the number you need, and try not to look ahead.

1 b) He demonstrated His glory and His disciples believed on Him.

3 c) That His body was a temple. He would die and arise from the grave after three days.

2 a) He drove the traders and moneychangers away.

Lesson 3

John 3

In this lesson you will study ...
Jesus and Nicodemus
The New Birth
Life for a Look
Jesus and John
He Who Comes from Heaven

JESUS AND NICODEMUS

Objective 1. *Explain the meaning of born again.*

Read John 3:1-21.

The New Birth

Read John 3:1-13 again.

Nicodemus was a teacher and a religious leader. He was well educated and lived a good life. He thought that the good things he did would please God and give him a place in heaven. Jesus told him, "No one can see the Kingdom of God unless he is born again."

Jesus explained that there are two kinds of life: natural life of the body and spiritual life. We are born with natural life, but we receive spiritual life from the Spirit of God. We have already learned in John 1:12 that we receive this new nature, we are born again, when we accept Jesus Christ as our Savior. God becomes our Father. We are born of God and become the children of God.

When anyone is joined to Christ he is a new being: the old is gone, the new has come (2 Corinthians 5:17).

Jesus said this new birth is "of water and of the Spirit." The Bible often uses figurative or picture language— words with a different meaning from what they usually have. "Water" here means the washing away of sin. This is a part of our salvation.

He saved us through the Holy Spirit, who gives us new birth and new life by washing us (Titus 3:5).

You have been made clean already by the teaching I have given you (John 15:3).

Spiritual cleansing comes from listening to and obeying the Word of God. When Jesus spoke of being born again of water, we believe He meant we are born again by hearing the Word of God and believing it.

For You To Do

1 What did Jesus tell Nicodemus?
   a) The good things he did would take him to heaven.
   b) No one can see the kingdom of God unless he is born again.

2 The new birth is
   a) being born of God by believing in Jesus and receiving Him as Savior.
   b) coming back to earth as another person after you die.
   c) being baptized in water.

Life for a Look

Read John 3:14-21 again.

Once, the people of God had sinned and were punished by being snakebitten. God loved them and told Moses to lift up a bronze snake where everyone

John 3

could see it. Whoever looked at it got well. Those who would not look died.

Everyone on earth has disobeyed God and has been condemned to die. But God loves us. He proved it by sending His Son to die for us. Jesus was lifted up on a cross like the snake made of bronze. Everyone who looks to Him—that is, believes in Him—is healed from the snakebite of sin. Those who will not believe in Him have to die in their sins. But those who look receive eternal life.

For You To Do

3 Memorize John 3:16. This is the best-loved verse in the Bible.

4 What is the greatest proof that God loves us?
a) He gave His Son to save us.
b) He gives us life.
c) He answers prayer.

JESUS AND JOHN

Objective 2. *Describe John the Baptist's understanding of who Jesus was.*

Read John 3:22-30.

The crowds that used to go to hear John the Baptist were now going to hear Jesus instead. Many of John's disciples had left him and were following Jesus. But John was not sad about this. God had sent him to tell people about Jesus. So he was happy when they left him to follow Jesus.

John's attitude and his words show what a noble, unselfish person he was. His words are a good motto for us. Jesus, and not John, was the one who really mattered in John's life.

He must become more important, while I become less important (John 3:30).

For You To Do

5 Memorize John 3:30.

6 Pray that Jesus may become more and more important every day in your life.

HE WHO COMES FROM HEAVEN

Read John 3:31-36.

In these verses John, the writer of the Good News, lets us know that Jesus is the one who comes from heaven. He is greater than anybody on earth or everybody on earth all put together. He is full of the Spirit of God. God loves Him and has given Him power over everything.

Whoever believes in the Son has eternal life; whoever disobeys the Son will not have life, but will remain under God's punishment (John 3:36).

Many verses in this chapter speak of eternal life. Eternal life is not living on and on in this world. It is God's never-ending life, the kind of life that Jesus had. Although Jesus died on the cross, His life did not end. He arose from the grave and He lives forever.

If we believe in Jesus, we have eternal life. Our bodies may die, but when they do, our spirits will go to God and will live with Him forever. And just as Jesus' body was raised from the dead, the bodies of those who believe in Him will one day be raised from the dead to enjoy eternal life.

For You To Do

7 What if we do not accept the salvation that God offers us in Jesus?
a) We may be saved by being baptized in water.
b) We may be saved after we die.
c) We will not be saved.

8 What if we do accept the salvation that God has provided through Jesus?
   a) Our bodies will never die.
   b) Our bodies may die, but we will go to live with God forever.
   c) Our bodies will never be raised from the dead.

9 Pray for any of your friends that do not believe in Jesus.

John 3

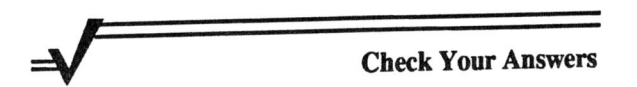

Check Your Answers

The answers to your study exercises are not given in the usual order, so that you will not see the answer to your next question ahead of time. Look for the number you need, and try not to look ahead.

4 a) He gave His Son to save us.

1 b) No one can see the kingdom of God unless he is born again.

7 c) We will not be saved.

2 a) being born of God by believing in Jesus and receiving Him as Savior.

8 b) Our bodies may die, but we will go to live with God forever.

Lesson 4

John 4

In this lesson you will study ...
Jesus and the Woman of Samaria
Jesus Heals an Official's Son

JESUS AND THE WOMAN OF SAMARIA

Objective 1. *Explain how Jesus was as living water to this woman.*

Read John 4:1-42.

Most people in Jesus' country looked down on the Samaritans, but Jesus loved everybody. He treated the rich, the poor, and people of different races all alike.

The woman of Samaria was very different from Nicodemus. Nicodemus was a good man, but he had to believe in Jesus before he could have eternal life. This woman was not good. Jesus knew that she was a bad woman, but He wanted to save her. Like Nicodemus, she too was saved by believing in Jesus.

Jesus let her know that He could give her the water of life—that she needed to satisfy the thirst of her spirit. In the Gospel of John the word "life" is used at least 36 times. Of these, it is joined 17 times with the word "eternal." We have learned that Jesus "had life in himself" (John 1:4); that those who believe in Jesus are born again and have eternal life (John 3:5, 15, 16, 36); that Jesus gives the water of life to those who accept it (John 4:14).

She spoke of her own customs of worship. Jesus said that places and customs of worship were not the most important things. What was important was that God is Spirit and people should worship Him as He really is.

Church membership and religious customs alone will not please God. God is never satisfied unless worship is true worship and spiritual worship. True worship must be what the Bible teaches. Spiritual worship must be sincere and according to the Holy Spirit.

The woman knew that Jesus was no ordinary man because He told her everything that she had done. When Jesus let her know that He was the Savior that God had promised to send into the world, she believed Him. She ran back to her village to tell all the people about Jesus. When she told them that the Messiah had come to their town, they hurried to the well to meet Him.

Jesus stayed with them two days, teaching them the way of salvation. The people said, "We believe now, not because of what you said, but because we ourselves have heard him, and we know that he is really the Savior of the world."

We must each one believe in Jesus and meet Him ourselves. The people first heard of Jesus from the woman. That was not enough. Perhaps you have heard of Jesus from your parents, from a pastor, or from a friend. But it is not enough just to hear about Jesus from others or to study about Him. You must meet Jesus personally in prayer and believe in Him as your own Savior.

John 4

For You To Do

1 Memorize John 4:24.

2 What did the villagers say about Jesus after He taught them?
   a) He was a good man who gave water to thirsty people.
   b) He was the Savior of the world.
   c) He was a prophet who knew all about people.

3 To be accepted by God, you must
   a) personally believe in Jesus as your own Savior.
   b) be born of Christian parents.
   c) hear about Jesus from a pastor or a friend.

JESUS HEALS AN OFFICIAL'S SON

Objective 2. *Explain how Jesus' healing of the official's son demonstrates His Lordship.*

Read John 4:43-54.

Have you ever asked Jesus to heal someone? An official asked Jesus to heal his son. Jesus did not go to the boy. He only told the father that the boy would get well, and the father believed the words of Jesus. It is a wonderful thing to know that Jesus still has the same power that He always had. We may be healed of sickness just by praying and believing Jesus' words.

For You To Do

4 How did Jesus heal the son of the government official?
   a) He sent some medicine.
   b) He made a magical charm.
   c) He said the boy would get well, and the father believed.

John 4

Check Your Answers

2 b) He was the Savior of the world.

4 c) He said the boy would get well, and the father believed.

3 a) Personally believe in Jesus as your own Savior.

Lesson 5

John 5

In this lesson you will study ...
The Healing at the Pool
The Authority of the Son
Witnesses to Jesus

THE HEALING AT THE POOL

Objective 1. *Explain the signigicance of Jesus' healing the man at the pool.*

Read John 5:1-18.

Chapter 5 tells of a man who had been sick for 38 years. There was a certain pool of water where people could be healed. However, whenever the water was

48

stirred up by an angel, only the first person to get into the pool was made well. This man could never get into the pool quickly enough to be healed. But Jesus healed him.

Some of the religious leaders were angry because Jesus healed this man on the Sabbath, or Saturday. They kept Saturday as a day of worship, and did not believe that any work should be done on that day. These leaders were thinking more about the fact that he was carrying his bed on the Sabbath than they were about the wonderful miracle that made him walk. They thought more about their traditions than about a man who needed help.

It is true that one day of the week should be kept for worship. But, it is always good to help people who need it. Jesus said, "My Father works always, and I too must work." If God did not work on every day of the week, we would all die.

For You To Do

1. Why was the helpless sick man waiting at the pool of Bethzatha?
   a) He wanted a drink of water.
   b) He wanted to be healed.
   c) He wanted to take a bath.

2. Why were the religious leaders angry?
   a) Because they were not paid money for the healing.
   b) Because the healing was not done by a doctor.
   c) Because Jesus healed a man on the Sabbath day.

3. How did Jesus answer the religious leaders?
   a) He told them He was working as His Father worked.
   b) He told them that healing was not working.
   c) He told them He had received permission from John the Baptist.

THE AUTHORITY OF THE SON

Objective 2. *Describe what authority God the Father has given to the Son.*

Read John 5:19-29.

John 5

God gave His Son Jesus the power and right to heal the sick, to raise the dead, to forgive sins, and even to judge the world. Verse 24 gives a wonderful promise that all who hear Jesus' words and believe in Him will not have to be judged for their sins. They have been saved from their sins and from the punishment of sin. They have received eternal life. They will not have to stand before Jesus and be condemned to die because they have believed in Him as Savior.

For You To Do

4 Memorize John 5:24.

5 Who will not have to be judged by Jesus for their sins?
  a) Those who have been members of a church.
  b) Those who have never done anything bad.
  c) Those who have heard Jesus' words and have believed in Him and in God.

WITNESSES TO JESUS

Objective 3. *Name two witnesses of Jesus.*

Read John 5:30-47.

This chapter speaks of the witnesses to Jesus. A witness to Jesus is someone or something that tells about Him and demonstrates who He is. All the witnesses in this chapter let us know that Jesus is the Son of God.

John the Baptist was one of these witnesses (verse 33). The works that Jesus did witnessed for Him (verse 36), giving proof that He was God's Son. The Father also gave witness (verse 37). Then the written Word of God was a witness (verse 39). Jesus is not an ordinary man. He is the one sent by the Father to give salvation and eternal life.

Check Your Answers

2 c) Because Jesus healed a man on the Sabbath day.

1 b) He wanted to be healed.

5 c) Those who have heard Jesus' words and have believed in Him and in God.

3 a) He told them He was working as the Father worked.

Lesson 6

John 6

In this lesson you will study ...
Jesus Feeds the Five Thousand
Jesus Walks on the Water
The People Seek Jesus
Jesus, the Bread of Life
The Words of Eternal Life

JESUS FEEDS THE FIVE THOUSAND

Objective 1. *Explain the lessons of the feeding of the 5,000.*

Read John 6:1-15.

Matthew, another of Jesus' disciples, tells us more about this miracle in chapter 14 of his gospel. Jesus and His disciples had gone to a lonely place to get away from the crowds. But the people followed Him, taking their sick with them so that He would heal them. And Jesus did heal them. Jesus had compassion on the people. It was late. Everyone was hungry and there was no place to get anything to eat.

Jesus taught us many lessons by what He did next. He let us see that God is interested in us and in our needs. He shows us that He can take care of our needs.

The word here translated "loaves" means very small loaves or buns. The five buns of bread and two small fish were just a good lunch for a hungry boy. But the Master asked for the bread and fish, and the boy let Him have it all. With Jesus' blessing this lunch became enough for the 5000 men to eat all they wanted. And the boy did not go hungry after all! He had all he could eat. We never lose by giving what we have to God. He always gives back to us more than what we give to Him.

It was after Jesus thanked God for what He had that the food was multiplied. As we thank God for what He has given us, He makes it enough to meet our needs. The disciples, too, helped in the miracle. As they received the broken food from Jesus' hands, it grew and multiplied to meet the need. The Word of God is sometimes called bread and meat. As we share His Word with others, God blesses it and makes it satisfy spiritually hungry persons.

Jesus always did things in an orderly way. He organized everything so that the great crowd could be fed without confusion. Then He had the disciples gather up what was left over, teaching that we should not be wasteful.

The people were excited by this miracle. The Messiah that God had promised to send them was going to be a prophet like Moses. Moses had prayed and God had given the people food called manna in the wilderness. Jesus, too, had miraculously fed a great crowd in the wilderness. He must be the Prophet, the Messiah. They wanted to make Him King.

But Jesus had not come to overthrow the Roman government and become the ruler of His country. He

John 6

had come to overthrow the power of sin in those who wanted to live right. He would become the Lord and King of many lives, but His kingdom was spiritual, not political. The people could not understand this, so He had to leave them.

For You To Do

1 Do you thank God for your food before you eat? .... Will you from now on?....................

2 What miracle did Jesus do with a boy's five loaves and two fish?
   a) He made enough food for the 12 disciples to eat.
   b) He made 12 baskets full of food.
   c) He made enough food to feed 5,000 men.

3 What did the people want to do after Jesus fed them?
   a) Repent of their sins and be saved.
   b) Crown Jesus king of their country.
   c) Accept Jesus as their spiritual ruler.

JESUS WALKS ON THE WATER

Objective 2. *Explain how the event of Jesus walking on the water shows Jesus as the Son of God.*

Read John 6:16-21.

Going back across Lake Galilee, the disciples were afraid because a storm was about to make their boat sink. Jesus walked on the water to them and got into the boat to save them. Who can walk on the water or stop a storm? Can any ordinary man? Jesus can do anything because He is the Son of God.

Having Jesus in the boat was like having Jesus in our lives. With Him we are safe in the storms of trouble. He takes away the fear and gives us peace. David, a songwriter of Bible times, wrote:

This poor man cried, and the Lord heard him, and saved him out of all his troubles (Psalm 34:6, KJV)

For You To Do

4 Has the Lord ever taken away your fears, given you peace, and delivered you out of trouble?

.... Thank Him for it.

THE PEOPLE SEEK JESUS

Read John 6:22-24.

Jesus was very popular. The crowds followed Him wherever He went. They thought that He was just the kind of person they needed for a king. With His miracle power He could heal all the sick. He would feed them and they would not have to work!

John 6 59

At that time Jesus' home was in the city of Capernaum on the western shore of the Sea of Galilee. The crowd that had wanted to make Him leader in a revolutionary movement followed Him there. But Jesus would not consider their offer. Later on His enemies accused Him of trying to stir up a revolution, but all the people knew how foolish that charge was.

For You To Do

5 Where was Jesus' home then?
 a) In Capernaum on the Mediterranean Sea.
 b) In Capernaum on the Sea of Galilee.
 c) In Nazareth.

JESUS, THE BREAD OF LIFE

Objective 3. *Explain what Jesus meant when He described himself as the bread of life.*

Read John 6:25-59.

Jesus taught that God wants people to believe in Him.

What God wants you to do is to believe in the one he sent (John 6:29).

They wanted Jesus to feed them manna. Jesus let them know that He had something better for them than manna. He was the Bread of Life that God had sent down from heaven.

Some of the people were angry when Jesus said that they must eat His flesh and drink His blood. This is another example of figurative language. Jesus meant that the people had to take Him into their lives just as they took food into their bodies. Food gave them physical life. He would give them eternal life.

At a later time Jesus gave His disciples bread and wine and told them that these represented His body and His blood. He told them to remember His death for them every time they ate together in this way. And so today we have what we call the Lord's Supper or Holy Communion. Taking communion does not save anyone. In fact, the Bible warns against taking communion unless you are first saved form sin.

For You To Do

6 Draw a line under the verse that you like best in this section.

7 Memorize John 6:29.

8 What did Jesus mean when He said, "If you do not eat the flesh of the Son of Man and drink his blood, you will not have life"?
   a) The people had to really eat His flesh.
   b) The people had to drink His real blood.
   c) The people had to take Him into their lives just like they took food when they ate.

9 What is the purpose of Holy Communion?
   a) It is to save us from sin.
   b) It is to show that we are members of the church.
   c)) It is to represent the body and the blood of Jesus; believers take communion to remember Jesus' death.

THE WORDS OF ETERNAL LIFE

Read John 6:60-71.

Some of those who start out to follow Jesus today get offended and turn away from Him. Jesus asked the disciples if they would leave Him. Peter said, "Lord, to whom would we go? You have the words that give eternal life." It is very important for us to understand the truth of what Peter said.

We must know Jesus to have eternal life, not just know about Him. You may know about the chief ruler of your country but not know him personally. Many persons know about Jesus without knowing Him personally as their Savior.

And eternal life means to know you, the only true God, and to know Jesus Christ, whom you sent (John 17:3).

Do you know Jesus as your own Savior? If not, you need to pray right now, confessing your sins and asking God to save you. Your hope of salvation must be, not in what you have done, but in what Jesus has done for you.

For You To Do

10 Memorize John 17:3.

11 What did Peter say?
   a) "Lord, to whom would we go? You have the words that give eternal life."
   b) "Lord, this teaching is too hard."
   c) "Lord, how can you give us your flesh to eat?"

12 What must you, yourself, do to be saved?
   a) You must believe that Jesus died for you and accept Him as your Savior.
   b) You must know about Jesus by hearing something about Him.
   c) You must get a good grade on this correspondence study course.

John 6

Check Your Answers

8 c) The people had to take Him into their lives just like they took food when they ate.

2 c) He made enough food to feed 5000 men.

9 c) It is to represent the body and the blood of Jesus; believers take communion to remember Jesus' death.

3 b) Crown Jesus king of their country.

11 a) "Lord, to whom would we go? You have the words that give eternal life."

5 b) In Capernaum on the Sea of Galilee.

12 a) You must believe that Jesus died for you and accept Him as your Savior.

Lesson 7

John 7

In this lesson you will study...
Jesus and His Brothers
Jesus at the Feast of Tabernacles
Is He the Messiah?
Guards Are Sent to Arrest Jesus
Streams of Living Water
Division Among the People
The Unbelief of the Jewish Leaders

JESUS AND HIS BROTHERS

Objective 1. *Explain the importance of patience in dealing with unbelievers.*

Read John 7:1-9.

This chapter tells about what different people thought about Jesus. Some did not want to believe in Him. Some were blinded by their own ideas that did not agree with Jesus' teaching. Some hated Him because He preached against the bad things that they did.

At this time Jesus' own brothers did not believe that He was the Messiah. Later they did. Many of Jesus' enemies were converted after His resurrection. Some of those who are enemies of the gospel now may accept Jesus if we pray for them. Jesus told His followers to love their enemies and to pray for them.

JESUS AT THE FEAST OF TABERNACLES

Objective 2. *Describe the three popular attitudes towards Jesus, and explain Jesus' teaching at the Feast.*

Read John 7:10-24.

Seven verses in this chapter tell us that Jesus was in danger. Read verses 1, 13, 19, 25, 30, 32, and 44. In spite of the danger, He kept on teaching and went to a religious celebration in Jerusalem. Many of Jesus' followers are in danger now. We should pray that God will give them courage to keep on teaching, preaching, or witnessing.

Jesus' teaching surprised the leaders. They knew that He had not attended their schools of higher education. The truths He taught came from God.

Read verse 17. If we are willing to do what God wants us to do, He will let us know the truth. Many persons who do not believe the gospel have this problem: they cannot recognize the truth because they are not willing to obey God. Even persons who did not believe that there was a God have found Him by praying sincerely: "God, if there is a God, please reveal Yourself to me. Let me know the truth and I will follow You."

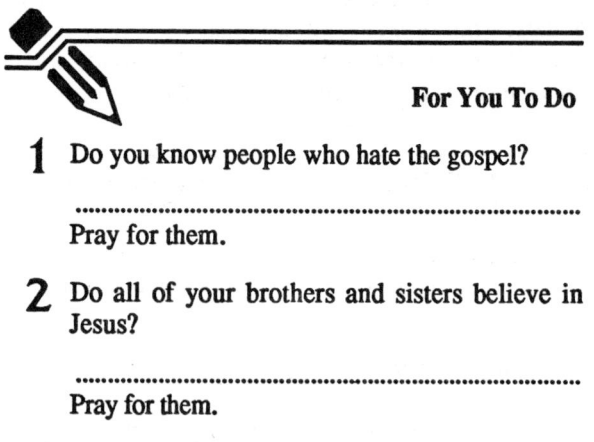

For You To Do

1 Do you know people who hate the gospel?

....
Pray for them.

2 Do all of your brothers and sisters believe in Jesus?

....
Pray for them.

Some were still complaining that Jesus had healed sick people on the Sabbath. One law sometimes seems to be against another. When this happens, Jesus taught that we should obey the most important one. For example, the law said that no work was to be done on the Sabbath; it said also that every male child was to be circumcised on the eighth day. If the eighth day was a Sabbath, the people broke the law of the Sabbath in order to keep the law of circumcision. Jesus taught that the law of kindness was more important than the law of the Sabbath.

For You To Do

3 Why was Jesus' teaching so great?
   a) Because He attended schools of higher education.
   b) Because the priests and the Pharisees were His teachers.
   c) Because His teaching was from God.

4 Pray for your unsaved friends that God will make them willing to give up their sins so that they can see the truth of the gospel.

5 Pray for those who are in danger because they are following Jesus.

IS HE THE MESSIAH?

Read John 7:25-31.

The people were surprised to see Jesus teaching in the temple because they knew that the religious leaders were trying to kill Him. But they could not kill Him until it was God's time for Him to die. Jesus knew that

God had sent Him and that God would help Him finish His work. So he kept on teaching right in the temple. Because He had the courage to do what God wanted Him to, many more persons believed in Him and were saved from their sins.

For You To Do

Fill in the blanks.

6 What did the leaders want to do to Jesus?
Kill him

7 Who had sent Jesus?
God

8 Is it always easy to do what God wants you to do?
No

9 Who will take care of you?
God

GUARDS ARE SENT TO ARREST JESUS

Objective 3. *Explain Jesus' climatic appeal and the response to it.*

Read John 7:32-36.

The fact that more people were believing on Jesus made the Pharisees more determined than ever to kill Him. Jesus knew that they were going to have Him killed. He had come to earth in order to die for our sins. He talked about His death as going away where they could not follow Him. His work would be over then. He would go back to heaven to be with God, His Father. Those who follow Jesus will go to heaven when they die.

For You To Do

10 How do we know Jesus had enemies?
   a) The chief priests wanted to kill Him.
   b) The Roman governor sent to have Him arrested.
   c) The crowds all wanted to kill Him.

STREAMS OF LIVING WATER

Read John 7:37-39.

Jesus said, "Whoever is thirsty should come to me and drink." We have already learned that Jesus compared salvation to the water of life. But verse 39 makes it clear that here the water was being compared to the Holy Spirit, who would be given to believers after they were saved. After a person is saved from his sins, he should desire to be filled with the Holy Spirit. In the book of Acts, we see that believers were filled with the Holy Spirit after they received Jesus as their Savior.

For You To Do

11 When Jesus said, "Whoever is thirsty should come to me and drink," what was He talking about?
   a) About salvation which He called the water of life.
   b) About the Holy Spirit who would be given to believers after they were saved.
   c) About the water from the Jordan River.

DIVISION AMONG THE PEOPLE

Read John 7:40-44.

People had different opinions about Jesus then, just as they do today. Those were right who said He was the Prophet that God had promised, the Messiah, the Son of God.

Jesus lived in the province of Galilee, but He had been born in Bethlehem. Both Luke and Matthew give us the list of Jesus' ancestors, showing that He was a descendant of David. He fulfilled the prophecies about the Messiah.

For You To Do

Fill in the blanks.

12 Where did the people say that the Messiah would be born?
Bethlehem

13 Where was Jesus born?
Bethlehem

14 Was Jesus a descendant of David?
Yes

THE UNBELIEF OF THE JEWISH LEADERS

Read John 7:45-52.

The Pharisees wanted to have Jesus arrested. One of the guards said, "Nobody has ever talked the way this man does!" No one could speak as Jesus did because no one else was God. We should learn what Jesus says about things and put His teachings above whatever anyone else says.

For You To Do

15 What did one of the guards testify about Jesus?
  a) "Nobody has ever talked the way this man does!"
  b) "No prophet ever comes from Galilee."
  c) "How does this man know so much when he has never been to school?"

Check Your Answers

10 a) The chief priests wanted to kill him.

3 c) Because His teaching was from God.

   11 b) About the Holy Spirit who would be given to believers after they were saved.

6 Kill Him.

   12 Bethlehem.

7 God.

   13 Bethlehem.

8 No.

   14 Yes.

9 God.

   15 a) "Nobody has ever talked the way this man does!"

Lesson 8

John 8

In this lesson you will study ...
The Woman Caught in Adultery
Jesus the Light of the World
You Cannot Go Where I am Going
Free Men and Slaves
Jesus and Abraham

THE WOMAN CAUGHT IN ADULTERY

Objective 1. *Explain Jesus' view of forgiveness of sins.*

Read John 8:1-11.

Jesus gave a very good rule about when to criticize and condemn others:

74

Whichever one of you has committed no sin may throw the first stone (John 8:7).

Possibly Jesus wrote the sins of which the men were guilty. They were ashamed and left.

Jesus was the only one there who had not sinned. He did not condemn the woman. He saved her life and forgave her sins. He told her to go and not to sin again. When God forgives us, we must not keep on sinning.

For You To Do

1 Memorize John 8:7. Whenever you feel like criticizing someone, quote this verse to yourself.

2 Pray that those who ask God for forgiveness will stop sinning.

JESUS THE LIGHT OF THE WORLD

Objective 2. *Explain what Jesus means by His self-description as the light of the world.*

Read John 8:12-20.

Jesus then told the people that He was the Light of the world. The Bible often speaks of the things of sin as darkness. Jesus, like a bright light, shows us our sins and He shows us the way to heaven also. We cannot go to heaven unless our sins are forgiven. Verse 24 says that those who do not believe in Jesus will die in their sins.

For You To Do

3 Go back to the introduction that John wrote for his Good News and read again John 1:1-9.

4 Why did Jesus call Himself the Light of the world?
   a) Because He is the true Light that will show us our sins and show us the way to heaven also.
   b) Because He always taught during the day and not at night.
   c) Because He gave everyone a lamp to use at night.

YOU CANNOT GO WHERE I AM GOING

Objective 3. *Explain the meaning of Jesus' statement, "Where I go, you cannot come."*

Read John 8:21-30.

Again Jesus talked to the people about His death as going where they could not follow Him. He had come from heaven and was going back to heaven. But first the Son of Man must be lifted up on a cross to die for the sins of the world. Remember how Jesus talked with Nicodemus about this back in chapter 3?

"I Am Who I Am" was the name that God used for Himself when Moses asked Him what His name was. It is Jesus' death and resurrection that makes us believe that He is our Savior.

For You To Do

5 Read three times verses 23, 24, 28, and 29.

6 Whom did Jesus tell that the Son of Man must be lifted up, even as Moses had lifted up the bronze snake on the pole in the desert?

Nicodemus

7 Read again John 3:14-21.

FREE MEN AND SLAVES

Objective 4. *Explain what Jesus means by slavery and freedom.*

Read John 8:31-47.

Jesus said that whoever sins is a slave of sin. A man who is a sinner cannot stop sinning even when he wants. Many have confessed that they do not know why they do the things they do, but they cannot seem to keep from doing them. A slave always has a master, and a sinner is the slave of the devil. But if we obey Jesus' teaching, He sets us free from sin and from the devil.

If you obey my teaching you are really my disciples; you will know the truth, and the truth will set you free. If the Son sets you free, then you will be really free (John 8:31, 32, 36).

For You To Do

8 Memorize John 8:31, 32, and 36.

9 Pray for any of your friends who are slaves to sin that they might find freedom in Jesus.

JESUS AND ABRAHAM

Objective 5. *Explain the signigicance of Jesus' words, "before Abraham was born, I am."*

Read John 8:48-59.

Some of the people who heard Jesus say these things were offended. They said that they had never been slaves. They were descendants of Abraham and were born free. We do not like to think that we are slaves of Satan, but this is a fact until Jesus makes us free.

When the Jews again spoke of Abraham, Jesus told them that Abraham was glad that he was to see Jesus' day. He said also, "Before Abraham was born, 'I Am.'" When He used the words, "I Am", in the present tense, He used the same words that God used in Exodus 3:14.

"And God said unto Moses, I AM THAT I AM: and he said, Thus shalt thou say unto the children of Israel, I AM hath sent me unto you"(Exodus 3:14, KJV).

This made some of the leaders so angry that they tried to stone Jesus. But Jesus left the temple in safety because it was not God's time for Him to die. It is true He came to die for our sins, but not before the time which God had set.

For You To Do

10 What did Jesus say about Himself and Abraham?
   a) "Abraham was also my father."
   b) "I have never seen Abraham."
   c) "Before Abraham was born, 'I Am.'"

Check Your Answers

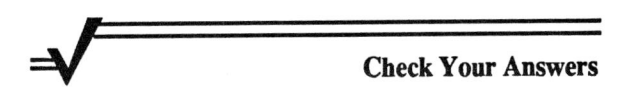

4 a) Because He is the true Light that will show us our sins and show us the way to heaven also.

10 c) "Before Abraham was born, 'I Am.'"

6 Nicodemus.

Lesson 9

John 9

In this lesson you will study ...
Jesus Heals a Man Born Blind
The Pharisees Investigate the Healing
Spiritual Blindness

JESUS HEALS A MAN BORN BLIND

Objective 1. *Explain how the healing of the man born blind shows the development of belief and unbelief.*

Read John 9:1-12.

The disciples believed that all sickness was a punishment for sin. But why should a man be born blind? It could not be because of his sin. He was born blind before he could do any wrong. Would it be because of the parents' sin?

Jesus let them know that sickness and suffering are not always the result of a person's sin. Many sicknesses come from natural causes and have nothing to do with sin and punishment. This man's blindness was going to give him an opportunity to be healed by Jesus and saved from his sins. Others would see God's power and believe on Jesus. So God, who knows all things before they happen, let the man be born blind.

Sometimes we cannot understand why we have to suffer. We try to correct any natural causes of sickness and take care of your health, but still we and our children suffer from accidents and disease. And we ask: "Lord, why has this happened to me?"

God does sometimes use suffering to correct us. We should search our heart and life and ask forgiveness of anything wrong that we have said or done, or any wrong attitudes and sinful thoughts. We should pray for God to heal us. Above all, let's pray that through our suffering others may see God's power and love and will praise Him. We want everything in our lives to bring glory to God.

For You To Do

1. Why was the man born blind?
   a) Because of his sins.
   b) Because of his parents' sins.
   c) So that God's power could be seen.

2. Why did the blind man not know who had healed him?
   a) He was not healed of his blindness until after he went to wash in the Pool of Siloam.
   b) When he was healed he did not ask Jesus who He was.
   c) He was a stranger in town.

THE PHARISEES INVESTIGATE THE HEALING

Read John 9:13-34.

Jesus' enemies were angry because He had healed the blind man on the Sabbath. They were not happy because the blind man had been healed. They tried to convince him that Jesus was a sinner and finally threw the healed man out of the synagogue (their church).

The man who had been healed set a good example for us. His arguments could not convince these

John 9

religious leaders that Jesus had come from God, but he could tell what Jesus had done for him. So can we.

One thing I do know: I was blind, and now I see (John 9:25)

For You To Do

3. Memorize John 9:25.
4. Pray God will help you tell others what Jesus has done for you.

SPIRITUAL BLINDNESS

Objective 2. *Explain the ultimate consequence of belief and unbelief.*

Read John 9:35-41.

It was a serious thing to be put out of the synagogue, almost like being declared dead. Jesus went to find the man to encourage him. He let the man know that He was the Savior. The man believed and worshiped Jesus.

Jesus spoke about spiritual blindness. The Pharisees were to blame for their spiritual blindness because they refused to accept the truth. But the blind beggar believed in Jesus and was both healed and saved from his sins.

If we do not want to be spiritually blind, we must accept Jesus as our personal Savior. Jesus comes to us and opens our eyes spiritually as we study the Bible and pray.

Open thou mine eyes, that I may behold wondrous things out of thy law (Psalm 119:18, KJV).

For You To Do

5 What other kind of blindness did Jesus talk about?
   a) Partial blindness when a person needs eyeglasses.
   b) The spiritual blindness of those who do not believe in Jesus.
   c) Color blindness.

6 What must each of us do to be healed of spiritual blindness?
   a) We must accept Christ personally and individually as our Savior.
   b) We must become a member of a church.
   c) We must have someone put mud on our eyes.

Check Your Answers

1. c) So that God's power could be seen.

5. b) The spiritual blindness of those who do not believe in Jesus.

2. a) He was not healed of his blindness until after he went to wash in the Pool of Siloam.

6. a) We must accept Christ personally and individually as our Savior.

Lesson 10: John 10

In this lesson you will study ...
The Parable of the Sheepfold
Jesus the Good Shepherd
Jesus Rejected by the Jews

THE PARABLE OF THE SHEEPFOLD

Objective 1. *Explain the meaning of the parable of the sheepfold.*

Read John 10:1-6.

A parable is a short story that uses natural things to explain spiritual truths. Jesus is the Good Shepherd who watches over His sheep and feeds them. His sheep are all those who believe in Him and follow Him. In Bible days a shepherd always walked in front of His sheep, calling them as He went. All the sheep knew His voice, and they followed him. When another shepherd came near with his sheep, the first man's sheep would not go after the second man because they knew the voice of their own shepherd.

For You To Do

1 Why did Jesus call Himself the Good Shepherd?
a) He owned many sheep.
b) He took good care of sheep and goats.
c) He takes care of those who belong to Him like a good shepherd takes care of his sheep.

JESUS THE GOOD SHEPHERD

Objective 2. *Explain the meaning of the parable of the Good Shepherd.*

Read John 10:7-21.

Jesus spoke of Himself as the door. In Bible lands a shepherd kept his sheep in a fenced corral or compound at night to protect them from wild animals. This was the sheepfold. After all the sheep were safe inside, the shepherd would sit down in the open door. He would protect the sheep. No wild animal could get in as long as he was there.

A thief would not try to enter by the door but would climb over the fence to steal a sheep if he could. Jesus said that some religious leaders were like that. They did not really love the people but only wanted to get what they could from them.

Jesus said that He did not come to destroy, but to give life; life in all its fullness. Life in all its fullness is a wonderful life here on earth and a never-ending life in heaven.

Jesus said, "I am the door. Whoever comes in by me will be saved." He did not say He was one of many doors, but that He was THE door [dash] the only door. Some people try to get to God through prophets, through saints, through Mary, or by joining a church. But Jesus is the only way, the only door (gate) to salvation.

Jesus said that a man had to come in. Just like the door was open for the sheep, Jesus invites everyone to come to Him and have eternal life. But God will not force anyone to come to Jesus and be one of His sheep. Each person must choose for himself. If a person comes into Jesus' sheepfold, he will be saved. If he does not enter, he will not be saved. It is just as simple as that.

Jesus said that He would give His life for His sheep. He would do this by His own choice; no one could take His life from Him. At that time certain people were trying to kill Him. There would come a day when He would be crucified: nailed to a cross made of wood and left there to die.

When the time came for Him to die, He would let His enemies kill Him. But He knew that death would not be the end for Him. He said, "I am willing to give

John 10   91

up my life, in order that I may receive it back again."
Jesus would come back to life and prove His power
over death. His resurrection would prove that He was
truly the Son of God.

Once again some of the people were angry at His
words, but others believed. Those who did not believe
were not His sheep, for His sheep would hear His
voice.

For You To Do

2. How many doors are there to salvation?
   a) There are many, for there are many religions by which we can be saved.
   b) There are at least four: Mary, the saints, the prophets, and the church.
   c) There is only one door, and that door is Jesus.

3. What do you have to do in order to be saved?
   a) You have to enter in order to be saved.
   b) You have to wait until someone opens the door.
   c) You do not have to do anything.

4. How did Jesus say He would show His love for His sheep?
   a) He would lead them to green pastures.
   b) He would give His life for His sheep.
   c) He would lead them beside quiet waters.

JESUS REJECTED BY THE JEWS

Objective 3. *Describe what is required of those who come to Jesus and what that means in terms of their belonging.*

Read John 10:22-42.

Some of the people wanted to kill Jesus because He said that He was the Son of God (verse 36) and gave eternal life to His followers (verse 28). Others accepted Him as their Good Shepherd and followed Him. You too must choose whether to follow Jesus or go your own way like a lost sheep.

For You To Do

5 When Jesus presented Himself as the Good Shepherd, how did the people receive Him?
a) Some wanted to kill Him; others followed Him.
b) They all rejected Him.
c) They all believed in Him.

6 Check your answers with those at the end of this lesson.

7 Now that you have completed the first ten lessons, you are ready to answer the first section of your student report. Review Lessons 1-10, then follow the instructions in your student report for filling out the answer sheet. Then return your answer sheet to the address given on the last page of the student report.

Check Your Answers

1. c) He takes care of those who belong to Him like a good shepherd takes care of his sheep.

4. b) He would give His life for His sheep.

2. c) There is only one door, and that door is Jesus.

5. a) Some wanted to kill Him; others followed Him.

3. a) You have to enter in order to be saved.

Lesson 11

John 11

In this lesson you will study...
The Death of Lazarus
Jesus the Resurrection and the Life
Jesus Weeps
Lazarus Brought to Life
The Plot Against Jesus

THE DEATH OF LAZARUS

Objective 1. *Explain why Jesus did not respond to the sister's plea immediately.*

Read John 11:1-16.

We have learned that Jesus had power over sickness. Now we see that He had power over death also. Today we know that doctors are trained to help sick people by giving them medicine. But no one has ever learned how to bring a dead man back to life. Jesus has this power within Him because He is God, the giver of all life.

Mary, Martha, and Lazarus lived in Bethany, about two miles from Jerusalem. When Lazarus became sick, his sisters sent a message to Jesus. Jesus did not go as soon as He received the message. This was not because He did not love Lazarus. It was because He knew what He was going to do. He knew that bringing Lazarus back to life would make people praise God more than just healing him of the sickness.

When Jesus said He would go to Bethany, His disciples tried to stop Him. Jesus' life had been in danger many times in Jerusalem, and the disciples were afraid for the Master.

Jesus again spoke of Himself as the Light of the world, saying that those who followed Him would not stumble in the darkness.

For You To Do

1 When Lazarus' sisters sent for Jesus, why did He not go at one to heal His friend?
   a) Jesus was too busy to worry about one sick man.
   b) Jesus was afraid to go to Jerusalem because His life was in danger.
   c) Jesus knew that Lazarus would die, but this would be a chance to show the power of God.

2 Have you ever wondered why your prayers were not answered right away?

....

Did it seem that Jesus did not care?

....

JESUS THE RESURRECTION AND THE LIFE

Objective 2. *Explain the meaning of Jesus' self-description as the resurrection and the life.*

Read John 11:17-27.

By the time Jesus got to Bethany, Lazarus had been dead and buried for four days. Martha ran to meet the Lord, saying, "If you had been here, Lord, my brother would not have died!" She said also that she knew God would give Jesus whatever He asked.

We see how Jesus led this woman to a greater belief in Himself. He first told her that her brother would rise again. Martha knew this, but she thought it would be in the resurrection of all the dead at the Judgment Day.

I am the resurrection and the life. Whoever believes in me will live, even though he dies (John 11:25).

Those who believe in Jesus will never die spiritually. And even if their bodies do die, they will live again when the time comes for their resurrection.

Martha said she believed that Jesus was the Son of God. Then Jesus went with Martha and others to Lazarus' grave. In those days the dead were usually buried in caves or in holes in the side of rocky hills. The dead body was placed inside and the opening to the cave was covered by a big rock.

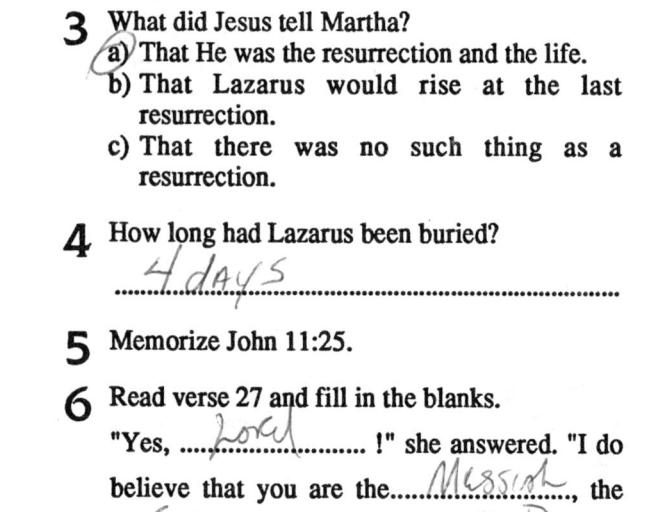

For You To Do

3 What did Jesus tell Martha?
   a) That He was the resurrection and the life.
   b) That Lazarus would rise at the last resurrection.
   c) That there was no such thing as a resurrection.

4 How long had Lazarus been buried?
   4 days

5 Memorize John 11:25.

6 Read verse 27 and fill in the blanks.
   "Yes, ...Lord...!" she answered. "I do believe that you are the ...Messiah..., the ...Son... of ...God..., who was to come into the world."

JESUS WEEPS

Objective 3. *Explain the significance of Jesus weeping.*

Read John 11:28-37.

Jesus is a real friend who cares when we have problems and sorrows. He wept with Martha and Mary and their friends but later He turned their sorrow to joy. We can take our grief to Him and find comfort.

Does Jesus Care

*Does Jesus care when my heart is pained
Too deeply for mirth or song,
As the burdens press, and the cares distress,
And the way grows weary and long?*

*Does Jesus care when I've said "goodbye"
To the dearest on earth to me,
And my sad heart aches till it nearly breaks,
Is it aught to Him? does He see?*

*O yes, He cares, I know He cares,
His heart is touched with my grief;
When the days are weary,
The long night dreary,
I know my Saviour cares.*

—*Frank E. Graeff*

For You To Do

7 Pray for anyone you know who needs Jesus' comfort for their sorrow.

LAZARUS BROUGHT TO LIFE

Objective 4. *Explain that Jesus' calling Lazarus from the tomb is an example of life through Christ conquering death.*

Read John 11:38-44.

What would Jesus do? All those standing near must have wondered. First Jesus prayed, thanking God for hearing Him. Then He commanded, "Lazarus, come out!" The dead man heard the voice of Jesus and came back from death to life.

This is a picture of the time when Jesus will call for all the dead to come out of their graves. The resurrection will be in two parts. Those who are saved will rise first. Much later the unsaved will come back to life and be judged for their sins.

The time is coming when all the dead will hear his voice and come out of their graves: those who have done good will rise and live, and those who have

John 11

done evil will rise and be condemned (John 5:28-29).

For just as all people die because of their union with Adam, in the same way all will be raised to life because of their union with Christ. But each one will be raised in his proper order: Christ, first of all; then, at the time of his coming, those who belong to him (1 Corinthians 15:22-23).

The rest of the dead did not come to life until the thousand years were over (Revelation 20:5).

For You To Do

8 What did Jesus do about Lazarus?
   a) He wept for Lazarus' death and that was all He could do.
   b) He called for Lazarus to come out of the grave, and Lazarus came back to life.
   c) He comforted Mary and Martha by telling them that their brother would be raised at the last resurrection.

9 Will all people who have died be raised from the dead?
   a) No, not all people will be raised from the dead —only good people.
   b) No, not all people will be raised from the dead —only bad people who will go to hell.
   c) Yes, all people will be raised from the dead: the good will be raised to life, and the bad will be condemned.

THE PLOT AGAINST JESUS

Read John 11:45-57.

The miracle of Lazarus being raised from the dead was reported to the religious leaders. Some of the leaders did not believe that there would ever be a resurrection at all. All the leaders feared that trouble would come to them from the Roman government, and they agreed to have Jesus put to death. Caiaphas the High Priest said it would be better for one man to die than for the whole nation to be destroyed.

For You To Do

10 What did the leaders think about Lazarus' resurrection?
   a) They praised God.
   b) They decided that Jesus must die.
   c) They did not believe that Lazarus had been dead.

Check Your Answers

1 c) Jesus knew that Lazarus would die, but this would be a chance to show the power of God.

   8 b) He called for Lazarus to come out of the grave, and Lazarus came back to life.

3 a) That He was the resurrection and the life.

   9 c) Yes, all people will be raised from the dead: the good will be raised to life, and the bad will be condemned.

4 Four days.

   10 b) They decided that Jesus must die.

6 Lord, Messiah, Son, God.

Lesson 12

John 12

In this lesson you will study...
Jesus Anointed at Bethany
The Plot Against Lazarus
The Triumphant Entry Into Jerusalem
Some Greeks Seek Jesus
Jesus Speaks About His Death
The Unbelief of the Jews
Judgment by Jesus' Word

JESUS ANOINTED AT BETHANY

Objective 1. *Explain the meaning of Mary's annointing of Jesus and Judas' reaction to it.*

Read John 12:1-8.

At Bethany a feast was prepared to celebrate the victory over death. Mary put some costly perfume on the feet of Jesus to show her love for Him. Judas at this

104

time showed that he was not a true disciple of Jesus. He said the perfume should have been sold and the money put into the money bag that he kept for all the disciples. He said that this would be used to feed the poor, but the truth was that he was a thief and wanted the money for himself.

For You To Do

1. What happened at dinner when they were celebrating the miracle?
   a) Judas stole some money from the bag that belonged to the disciples.
   b) Mary anointed Jesus' feet and Judas said the perfume should have been sold.
   c) Judas showed he was not a true disciple by not going to the feast at all.

THE PLOT AGAINST LAZARUS

Read John 12:9-11.

Many people came to see Lazarus when they heard that he had been raised from the dead. Through this miracle, many people believed in Jesus.

Satan, the devil, is God's enemy and he stirs people up to fight against God. He stirred the religious leaders up to fight against Jesus. They wanted to destroy Lazarus because he was living proof that Jesus really was the resurrection and the life. Many people believed in Jesus because of His testimony. Satan still wants to destroy those who tell others about Jesus' power.

For You To Do

2 Why did the religious leaders decide to kill Lazarus?
   a) Because many people believed on Jesus through Lazarus' testimony.
   b) Because Lazarus lived in Bethany.
   c) Because Lazarus had broken the law.

THE TRIUMPHANT ENTRY INTO JERUSALEM

Objective 2. *Explain the importance of Jesus' entry into Jerusalem.*

Read John 12:12-19.

It was the time of the Passover, a yearly feast to remind the people how God had saved them from slavery and from death. Many people went to Jerusalem at this time, as the center of worship for God's people was there.

Jesus went to Jerusalem for the Passover. The people waved palm branches before Him as He rode into town on a young donkey. They did this to honor Him as their Messiah and king. Some of them called Him King of Israel. Afterwards, when Jesus was arrested, His enemies used this against Him. They accused Him of trying to be king.

Today we should all look at Jesus as our king—not an earthly or political king, but the king of our own lives. A king is a ruler, and Jesus must rule our lives. And so we always try to do what He wants us to do. One of the things that brings shame upon the church today is that many members go to the services in the church, but outside the church they never try to do what Jesus taught. Jesus must be king of our lives wherever we are: in school, in the market, at the job, everywhere.

For You To Do

3 What was the Passover?
  a) It was a feast to remind people how God had saved them from slavery.
  b) It was a time when persons who lived far away passed over to Jerusalem to hold a political congress.
  c) It was a time when people celebrated the birth of the baby Jesus.

4 What happened when Jesus went to Jerusalem at this time?
  a) He taught people the meaning of the Passover.
  b) He rode on a young donkey to visit His friends.
  c) People welcomed Him and called Him King of Israel.

5 How should Jesus be king today?
  a) He should be king of the country where we live.
  b) He should be king of our lives and rule our lives.
  c) He should be king in the church but not outside.

SOME GREEKS SEEK JESUS

Objective 3. *Explain how Jesus' response to the request of the Greeks is a call to discipleship.*

Read John 12:20-26.

John 12

Some Greeks also went to see Jesus. Jesus knew that in a few days He would be crucified, nailed to a cross like a criminal. But because of His death, not only Greeks but persons from every country would be saved. They would have Him as their king forever. This was worth dying for. He would be like the grain of wheat that gives up its life to produce many more grains.

A grain of wheat remains no more than a single grain unless it is dropped into the ground and dies. If it does die, then it produces many grains (John 12:24-25).

Jesus said that we must follow Him. We must be willing to give up our lives for His sake so that others may receive Him and be saved.

For You To Do

6 Memorize John 12:24-25.

7 Pray that you may follow Jesus faithfully even if it means dying for His sake.

JESUS SPEAKS ABOUT HIS DEATH

Objective 4. *Explain how Jesus' hour, the hour of the cross, changes things.*

Read John 12:27-36.

How would you feel if you knew that within a few hours you were going to be put to death for crimes that you had not done? How would you pray?

This was Jesus' experience. He wanted to pray for God to save Him from such suffering. But He knew that He had come from heaven to earth and had become a man for this very purpose. He was going to die for the sins of the whole world—for your sins and mine. So He prayed: "O Father, bring glory to your name!"

What help it was to Jesus when God answered Him from heaven in a voice that all could hear. God was with Him. God would help Him go through the terrible hours ahead. And through His death God's name would be praised and glorified.

At Jesus' death sin was judged. Satan was judged. And your sins were judged. Jesus took your sins and the judgment for your sins upon Himself. Yet it is true that if you do not accept what He did for you, you will have to stand before God in judgment yourself and be punished for your sins.

Suppose you owed a great debt but someone paid it for you. How foolish it would be for you to try to pay it again! Jesus paid a great debt for you when He died for your sins. But to get the benefit of His payment you must accept Him as Savior and Lord.

For You To Do

8 What did Jesus do about sin when He died?
   a) He took all sin upon Himself and all people are free from sin.
   b) He took people's sin upon Himself but they will have to be punished for sin anyway.
   c) He took sin upon Himself, but only those who believe in Him will be free from punishment for sin.

THE UNBELIEF OF THE JEWS

Objective 5. *Describe the three characteristics of a true believer in verses 42 - 47.*

Read John 12:37-43.

Many of the people did not believe that Jesus was the Messiah because He did not fit their ideas of what the Messiah would do. But even their unbelief fit right into the picture that the prophet Isaiah had given of the Messiah.

Many of the leaders saw that Jesus was the Messiah but were afraid to accept Him because of what the others would do to them. Many persons today are afraid to become Christians for the same reason. Some are secret believers.

They loved the approval of men rather than the approval of God (John 12:43).

For You To Do

9. Memorize John 12:43.

10. Pray for those who are secret believers in Jesus.

JUDGMENT BY JESUS' WORD

Read John 12:44-50.

The very words that they refused to listen to would be the words by which they would be judged at the last judgment. Whoever believes Jesus' words and does what He tells them to do will be all right. The ones who do not believe what Jesus has said will not have eternal life.

For You To Do

11. By what will people be judged at the last judgment?
    a) They will be judged by Jesus' words.
    b) They will be judged by the laws of the country where they live.
    c) They will be judged by the Ten Commandments.

Check Your Answers

1 b) Mary anointed Jesus' feet and Judas said the perfume should have been sold.

   5 b) He should be king of our lives and rule our lives.

2 a) Because many people believed on Jesus through Lazarus' testimony.

   8 c) He took sin upon Himself, but only those who believe in Him will be free from punishment for sin.

3 a) It was a feast to remind people how God had saved them from slavery.

   11 a) They will be judged by Jesus' words.

4 c) People welcomed Him and called Him King of Israel.

Lesson 13

John 13

In this lesson you will study ...
Jesus Washes His Disciples' Feet
Jesus Predicts His Betrayal
The New Commandment
Jesus Predicts Peter's Denial

JESUS WASHED HIS DISCIPLES' FEET

Objective 1. *Explain how Jesus' washing of the disciples' feet showed the full extent of His love.*

Read John 13:1-20.

At the Passover, lambs were sacrificed for the sins of the people. So on the day of the Passover, Jesus, the Lamb of God, was going to die for the sins of the world. But first He must teach His disciples a lesson. They had been arguing over who would be greatest in His kingdom. Jesus wanted to teach them that true greatness is to serve others.

It was the custom for a servant to wash the feet of the guests. Or one friend might honor another by washing his feet. But not one of the disciples was willing to do the work of a servant and wash the feet of the others. So Jesus washed their feet!

How ashamed they were! Jesus, the Son of God, was doing the work that they had thought they were too good to do! Their Master was taking the place of a slave to make them more comfortable! If we are going to follow Jesus, we must be willing to humble ourselves and do whatever needs to be done to help others. This is our way of "washing their feet."

Jesus taught another lesson: we must let Him cleanse us daily from our faults. The disciples had bathed just before going to the place where they ate, but they had gotten their feet dirty walking along the dusty streets. Getting saved is like taking a bath. When we accept Jesus as our Savior, He washes away all our sins; they are gone forever and forgotten. But day by day, as we walk through life, we sometimes "get our feet dirty." We do things we should not do. We do not need to get saved all over again but we must take our faults and failures to Jesus and let Him wash them away.

For You To Do

1 What did Jesus do to teach His disciples that they should serve one another?
  a) He took a servant's place and washed their feet.
  b) He told how He had left heaven to become a man.
  c) He served the food to the disciples.

2 Do you have faults that you want to get rid of?

.... Talk with Jesus about them.

JESUS PREDICTS HIS BETRAYAL

Objective 2. *Explain the significance of Judas' going out into the night.*

Read John 13:21-30.

Jesus knew how He would be betrayed. Judas, one of His own disciples, would turn against Him. One trouble Judas had was his love of money. He was treasurer and stole from the general funds. This may seem like a little thing but one sin leads to another. Judas turned Jesus over to His enemies for thirty pieces of silver. He sold his own soul, his place in Christ's kingdom.

For the love of money is a source of all kinds of evil (1 Timothy 6:10).

For You To Do

3 Did Jesus expect to be betrayed?
   a) No, He did not.
   b) Yes, but He did not know who would betray Him.
   c) Yes, He knew Judas was going to betray Him.

4 Pray for your friends that none of them will lose their souls because of their love for money.

THE NEW COMMANDMENT

Objective 3. *Describe Jesus' new commandment.*

Read John 13:31-35.

Jesus again told His disciples of His death, that He would go where they could not go at that time. They had to stay on earth and live in such a way that all men would know they had something different about them. They were to love one another, even as He loved them. This is still a very important command that we must follow daily.

For You To Do

5. What was the new commandment that Jesus gave His disciples?
   a) They were to wash one another's feet every day.
   b) They were to love one another.
   c) They should not steal from the money bag.

JESUS PREDICTS PETER'S DENIAL

Read John 13:36-38.

You have already learned that Jesus was the Prophet that God had promised. God shows prophets things that are going to happen. Then the prophets predict these events, or tell about them before they happen, You have read several of Jesus' predictions. He said that He would be "lifted up," crucified; Judas would betray Him, and Peter would deny that he knew Him.

Peter thought he was stronger spiritually than the other disciples. Jesus knew how weak he was and was praying for him.

For You To Do

6 Jesus predicted that Peter would
a) be head of the church.
b) always be true to Him.
c) deny Him three times.

Check Your Answers

1 a) He took a servant's place and washed their feet.

   5 b) They were to love one another.

3 c) Yes, He knew Judas was going to betray Him.

   6 c) deny Him three times.

Lesson 14: John 14

In this lesson you will study...
Jesus the Way to the Father
The Promise of the Holy Spirit

JESUS THE WAY TO THE FATHER

Objective 1. *Explain the meaning of Jesus' self-description as the way and the truth and the life.*

Read John 14:1-14.

When Jesus told His followers that He would die and leave them, they were very sad. Jesus encouraged them by saying that He was going to prepare a place for them. Later He would come again and take them to be with Him.

It is very important for us to remember that Jesus will come back again for His own people. He will take them all to be with Him forever. That will be a wonderful day and we all should get ready for it. If our lives have sin in them, Jesus will not take us with Him. If we are saved from our sins and are living for God, then we will be taken to be with the Lord.

And after I go and prepare a place for you, I will come again and take you to myself, so that you will be where I am (John 14:3).

Jesus repeated that He is the only way to the Father. There are no other ways to get to heaven. You must believe in the Lord Jesus Christ to be saved, and only in Him.

I am the way, the truth, and the life; no one goes to the Father except by me (John 14:6).

Jesus promised that those who believed in Him would do greater works than they had seen Jesus do. Jesus could be in only one place at a time. But when His followers increased to many thousands, all of them could by the help of God do even more than Jesus did.

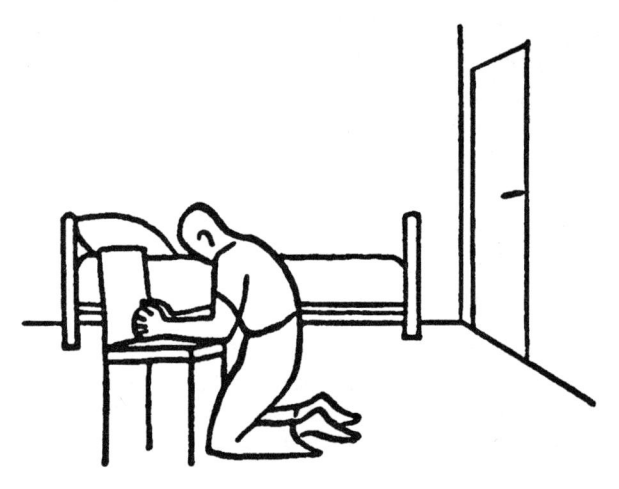

Jesus also said that we could pray in His name (verse 13-14). Asking in Jesus' name means praying the kind of prayers that Jesus Himself would pray. It means understanding God's will and praying for those things which are according to His will. Also, it means praying with the authority that Jesus had.

Sickness and evil spirits were cast out when Jesus spoke with authority. We can expect the great works that verse 12 speaks about only when we pray in the authority of Jesus' name. We do not have any authority in ourselves.

For You To Do

1. Memorize John 14:3, John 14:6.

2. How did Jesus encourage His disciples after saying He would leave them?
   a) He said He would come back to take them to be with Him.
   b) He said they also would die and go to be with God.
   c) He said they would not need Him any more.

3. How many ways are there to God?
   a) Many. Any religion will take you to God.
   b) Any way you follow is all right if you are sincere.
   c) One way—Jesus Christ.

4. What did Jesus say about prayer?
   a) His followers should pray in His name and He would do what they asked.
   b) His followers should pray in Mary's name, for she was Jesus' mother.
   c) His followers should pray to images.

THE PROMISE OF THE HOLY SPIRIT

Objective 2. *Explain the nature and the work fo the Holy Spirit.*

Read John 14:15-31.

In chapters 14, 15, and 16 we read about the things that the Holy Spirit does as our Helper. The people of the world cannot receive the Holy Spirit, but believers do receive. He is the Spirit of Truth who helps us know the truth. He teaches us and helps us remember and understand what Jesus taught.

I will ask the Father, and he will give you another Helper, who will stay with you forever (John 14:16).

Jesus said that what we do proves whether we love Him or not.

Whoever loves me will obey my teaching. My Father will love him, and my Father and I will come to him and live with him (John 14:23).

Many people think the commandments of Jesus are too hard. When God and Jesus live with us, they help us. With their help we can do everything that they tell us to do.

For You To Do

5 Memorize John 14:16, 23.

6 What help did Jesus promise the disciples after He went away?
a) He would send the Holy Spirit to stay with them.
b) He would pray for them.
c) He would talk with them.

7 What test is there for those who say they love Jesus?
   a) They go to church and are baptized in water.
   b) They obey His teaching.
   c) They do good deeds.

Check Your Answers

2 a) He said He would come back to take them to be with Him.

6 a) He would send the Holy Spirit to stay with them.

3 c) One way—Jesus Christ.

7 b) They obey His teaching.

4 a) His followers should pray in His name and He would do what they asked.

Lesson 15

John 15

In this lesson you will study...
Jesus the Real Vine
The World's Hatred

JESUS THE REAL VINE

Objective 1. *Explain the meaning of Jesus as the vine and believers as the branches.*

Read John 15:1-17.

Jesus compares Himself to a grapevine and His followers to the branches. His life in us produces what we sometimes call the fruit of the Spirit. This is the kind of fruit that God, the gardener, looks for in us.

But the Spirit produces love, joy, peace, patience, kindness, goodness, faithfulness, humility, and self-control (Galatians 5:22-23).

Every so often the gardener has to prune or trim the vine. He cuts away the old bushy growth to make the branches put out the new little branches that bear the grapes.

Jesus said that the disciples were clean by His Word. God uses the Bible as His pruning knife to cut away such things as our selfishness, pride, and bad temper. As we read the Bible, believe it, and accept it as the pattern for our lives, the Holy Spirit helps us get rid of the fruitless brush. Then the abundant life of Christ, like the sap flowing from the trunk into the branches, brings rapid spiritual growth and produces the fruit of the Spirit.

The word "remain" is repeated several times in this chapter: verses 4, 5, 6, 7, 9, and 10. This is very important. If a branch does not stay in the tree, or vine, it will die because its life comes from the trunk. In the same way, our spiritual life depends on our being joined to Jesus Christ. As long as we stay in Him, we will have life. But if we let anything turn us away from Jesus and back to sin, then we will no longer have life.

I am the vine, and you are the branches. Whoever remains in me, and I in him, will bear much fruit; for you can do nothing without me (John 15:5).

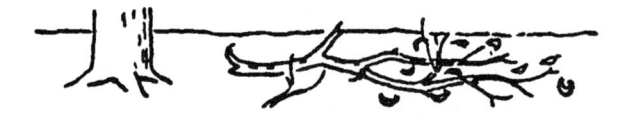

We see in this chapter that the relationship between the believers and Jesus is one of love. The word "love" is used over thirty times in chapters 13 through 17. First Jesus told how the Father loved Him; then how He loved the disciples. The disciples are to *continue* in His love.

As we stay in Jesus, He will help us love one another. Sometimes we say we could love certain persons if they were better. But Jesus did not love us because we were lovable people. He loved us and died for us while we were sinners. He chose us to let the world see His life and His love in us. Read verse 16.

For You To Do

1. Memorize Galatians 5:22-23 and John 15:5.

2. To what did Jesus compare Himself and His disciples?
   a) A farm and its fruit.
   b) A vine and its branches.
   c) A master and his slaves.

3. What does Jesus' message do?
   a) It makes us clean as we accept it and obey it.
   b) If we read it our lives will automatically become clean.
   c) It does not do anything.

4. What can we do without Jesus?
   a) Greater things than He did.
   b) Bear much fruit.
   c) Nothing.

5. What is the basis for the relationship between believers and Jesus?
   a) Love.
   b) Church membership.
   c) Good works.

THE WORLD'S HATRED

Objective 2. *Explain the reason for persecution.*

Read John 15:18-27 and John 16:1-4.

Jesus tells of persecution and misunderstanding that the disciples would suffer in the world. Of the eleven disciples to whom Jesus spoke these words, ten would be put to death for preaching the gospel. John was the only one to die a natural death.

Why does the world hate those who follow Jesus? For the same reason that it hated Him. The good life of a true Christian shows up the sinfulness around him. It makes the sinners feel guilty. This makes them dislike the Christian and they do whatever they can against him.

Then Satan, the enemy of God, fights against Christians. He stirs up people to make fun of Christians and to treat them badly. So do not be surprised if people make fun of you, or if they persecute you because you belong to Christ. Some Christians have been beaten by their families. Some have been put in jail. Others have even been put to death for having accepted Christ as their Savior.

Jesus said that His followers are not better than He is. The world persecuted Him and it will persecute all those who follow Him.

Again Jesus promised a Helper—the Holy Spirit. The Holy Spirit would speak more about Jesus and also help the disciples to speak about Jesus.

For You To Do

6 Pray for those who are suffering persecution.

7 What promise of a helper did Jesus again give?
   a) He promised them friends who would help them.
   b) He promised them farmers who would give them fruit from the vines.
   c) He promised them the Holy Spirit.

Check Your Answers

2 b) A vine and its branches.

5   a) Love.

3 a) It makes us clean as we accept it and obey it.

7   c) He promised them the Holy Spirit.

4 c) Nothing

Lesson 16: John 16

In this lesson you will study...
The Work of the Holy Spirit
Sadness and Gladness
Victory Over the World

THE WORK OF THE HOLY SPIRIT

Objective 1. *Describe the work of the Holy Spirit.*

Read John 16:4-15.

Five times during the last supper that Jesus had with His disciples, He spoke of the Holy Spirit. Read John 14:16-17, 26; 15:26; 16:7-15. In the first three verses the Father, Jesus, and the Holy Spirit are included together so that we understand that the three are really one God.

The word translated "Helper" here is the Greek word "Paraclete." This means a counselor or lawyer called to defend a person on trial; someone who is with a person to help and advise him. The Holy Spirit does this for us. He defends us. He advises us what to do. He is the Spirit of Truth who teaches us and leads us into all truth. He keeps us from being deceived by false teachers.

He lets the world know that it is wrong to sin. It is hard for us to admit that we are sinners. We think we are pretty good until the Holy Spirit shows us what we look like to God. Have you ever been surprised to see that the shirt or dress that you were wearing had stains on it? In the house it looked clean, but out in the bright light you could see the stains. The Holy Spirit turns God's bright light onto our lives and shows us how dirty our sins are.

For You To Do

1 What is the Greek word translated here as "Helper?"
   a) Parenthesis
   b) Paraclete
   c) Paralysis

2 As the Paraclete, what does the Holy Spirit do?
   a) He defends, advises, and helps us.
   b) He does our work for us.
   c) He accuses us.

3 When can we really see that we are sinners?
   a) When we get caught.
   b) When the Holy Spirit shows us how bad we are.
   c) When someone tells us bad we are.

4 Pray that you will always let the Holy Spirit guide you. Ask Him to show you anything in you that is not right.

SADNESS AND GLADNESS

Objective 2. *Explain the power of praying in Jesus' name.*

John 16:16-24.

The disciples were sad because Jesus was going to leave them. But Jesus gave them a wonderful promise for all His followers.

The Father will give you whatever you ask of him in my name (John 16:23).

If we were to ask and important person for something, we would not receive it because he would not know us. But if we were given the right to ask in the name of the head of our nation, everyone would quickly run to get what we asked for. God the Father will surely do what His Son asks. When we let Jesus live in us, we can pray in His name for the same things He would pray for. Then we can be sure of the answer.

For You To Do

5 What did Jesus promise?
  a) We can have anything we want.
  b) God will give us what we ask in Jesus' name.
  c) We will never be sad.

VICTORY OVER THE WORLD

Objective 3. *Explain how we can have peace even in the midst of trouble.*

Read John 16:25-33.

Jesus knew that in a few hours He would be arrested and all His disciples would run away to save their lives. He let them know what was going to happen. He wanted them to know that His suffering and death were not defeat. They were part of God's plan. It was through His suffering and death that souls could be saved.

The world would say: "Forget about others; save yourself!" But Jesus had overcome the world's temptations. He was doing what God wanted Him to do. Doing what God wants us to do, whatever it costs, is victory over the world.

The disciples too were going to suffer. Jesus reminded them to stay in Him and He would help them. All those who follow Jesus will face problems and suffering in this world but the Holy Spirit will be our Helper. Our victory is not in what we can do for ourselves but in what He does for us. He is with us to give us courage, strength, and peace in times of suffering. Our suffering for Jesus will be for only a little while, then we will reign with Him in eternal joy —no more suffering forever.

> I have told you this so that you will have peace by being united to me. The world will make you suffer. But be brave! I have defeated the world (John 16:33).

For You To Do

6 Read John 16:33 five times.

7 What does the world say?
a) "Forget yourself. Save others!"
b) "Save yourself and others too!"
c) "Forget others. Save yourself!"

John 16

8 What did Jesus say the world would do to His followers?
   a) Make them rulers.
   b) Make them suffer.
   c) Accept them as teachers.

9 What is victory for those who follow Jesus?
   a) Having their own way.
   b) Escaping from trouble.
   c) Doing God's will whatever it costs.

Check Your Answers

5 b) God will give us what we ask in Jesus' name.

1 b) Paraclete.

   7 c) "Forget others. Save yourself!"

2 a) He defends, advises, and helps us.

   8 b) Make them suffer.

3 b) When the Holy Spirit shows us how bad we are.

   9 c) Doing God's will whatever it costs.

Lesson 17: John 17

In this lesson you will study ...
Jesus Prays for His Disciples
The Men You Gave Me
Keep Them Safe
May They Be One
To Be With Me

JESUS PRAYS FOR HIS DISCIPLES

Read John chapter 17.

The Men You Gave Me

Objective 1. *Describe what Jesus prayed for concerning the disciples.*

Read John 17:1-8 again.

John chapter 17 is the prayer that Jesus prayed for His followers just before He was arrested. He had finished His work of teaching and preaching. Through Him His followers had gotten acquainted with God. He had given them eternal life.

And eternal life means to know you, the only true God, and to know Jesus Christ, whom you sent (John 17:3).

The time had come for Jesus to die for the sins of the world. He presented to His Father the men that God had given Him out of the world. They still lived in the world but were no longer a part of its wicked, ungodly system. They lived for God instead of worldly pleasure, power, or fame.

For You To Do

1 Memorize John 17:3.

Keep Them Safe

Read John 17:9-20 again.

Jesus spoke of the men God had given Him out of the world. The disciples of Jesus were not born as saints, or holy men. They were sinners just the same as other men. But they turned from their sins to believe in Jesus Christ and follow Him. And so they were saved.

Jesus knew that He would leave His followers that very night. He prayed for God to keep them safe. One of the disciples, Judas, was lost even while Jesus was with them. Jesus knew that after He left the disciples, they would all be tempted to give up what He had taught them and to go back to their old life.

Satan cannot take us away from God, but he does try to get us to turn away from God and go back into sin. After you decide to live for Christ, Satan will tempt you to go back. Remember that Jesus has prayed for you and is praying for you now. Read verse 20.

> And so he is able, now and always, to save those who come to God through him, because he lives forever to plead with God for them (Hebrews 7:25).

Jesus does not ask the Father to take us out of the world so that we will not have to suffer. We have work to do. He has sent us into the world with the message of salvation.

Several times in this chapter, Jesus taught that He gave His followers the true Word of God: verses 8, 14, 17. In verse 17 we are told that we are to be God's own by means of His Word.

Jesus said also that He sent His followers into the world just as God had sent Him. Jesus came to seek and to save the lost. So we as Christians should try to win other people to the Lord. We must keep on giving them the Word of God in churches, schools, literature, radio, and personal witnessing. And we must live a true Christian life before them to show them the way of life.

For You To Do

2 How does Satan treat Christians?
  a) He leaves them alone.
  b) He tries to get them to leave God and return to sin.
  c) He takes them away from God.

3 How should we act toward the world?
  a) We should pray to leave it.
  b) We should live in it and enjoy its pleasure.
  c) We should give God's Word to the world.

4 How are Jesus' followers to be sent into the world?
  a) As sheep without a shepherd because Jesus has gone.
  b) As God sent Jesus: to look for the lost and win them for the Lord.
  c) As church members to ask people to join their church.

May They Be One

Objective 2. *Describe what Jesus prayed for concerning those that would believe.*

Read John 17:20-33 again.

Jesus was praying not only for His disciples who lived at that time but for all who would believe in Him. That means you. Jesus prayed that all His followers would be one. This means that He wanted them to live and work together in unity. It is not good for Christians to be divided and work against one another.

There are many different churches, but the members can live in peace if they are willing to put Christ first. Some people today say that all churches should become one church, but this can never be done as long as the different churches believe different things.

We cannot join with a church that does not believe what Jesus taught. We believe that Jesus is the Son of

John 17

God, born of the Virgin Mary, and that His death for us is the only thing that can save us from sin. We must agree on these important things if we are to "be one."

> Can two walk together, except they be agreed? (Amos 3:3, KJV).

Jesus prayed that we might be one in Him and in the Father. Being in Christ is basic to Christian unity. If you want Christian fellowship and spiritual help, join a church that believes, teaches, and obeys the Bible—a church where Christ's presence is real.

For You To Do

5 For whom was Jesus praying?
   a) For the twelve disciples.
   b) For all church members that they would join the same church.
   c) For all those who believe in Him, even those who believe today.

6 Does it make you happy to know that Jesus prays for you? .... Thank Him for His prayers.

7 When Jesus prayed for His followers to be one, did He mean that all Christians should belong to one church today?
   a) Yes, there should not be different churches.
   b) No, Christians should not belong to a church.
   c) No, for some churches do not believe the very things that Jesus taught.

8 Pray for unity among Christians.

To Be With Me

Read John 17:24-26 again.

Jesus closed His prayer by saying that He wanted His followers to be with Him wherever He was. One day we will go to be with Him. The book of Revelation (the last book in the Bible) tells of all the saved ones standing before the throne of God and singing praise to Jesus, the Lamb that was slain.

We do not know when we will be called to go to be with the Lord. Until then we must live every day in a way to please God. Then we will not fear death, for we will know that death is only a door through which we will enter into God's presence.

Jesus will take only saved people to be with Him. Unsaved people will never have a place with Him. Do you want to be with Jesus forever?

There will be the shout of command, the archangel's voice, the sound of God's trumpet, and the Lord himself will come down from heaven! Those who have died believing in Christ will be raised to life first; then we who are living at that time will all be gathered up along with them in the clouds to meet the Lord in the air. And so we will always be with the Lord. So then, encourage one another with these words (1 Thessalonians 4:16-18).

John 17

For You To Do

9 How did Jesus close His prayer?
   a) By saying that He wanted His followers to be with Him wherever He was.
   b) By saying He might give people a chance to be saved after they die.
   c) By saying that the world knew God.

10 If you should die today, would you go to be with the Lord?
   a) I am not sure.
   b) No, for I am not saved.
   c) Yes, for I have believed in Jesus as my own savior.

If you cannot circle c), you should stop right now and pray, asking Jesus Christ to cleanse your sins and to save you. Then you, too, will be sure to go to be with the Lord when your life is over.

Check Your Answers

5 c) For all those who believe in Him, even those who believe today.

2 b) He tries to get them to leave God and return to sin.

  7 c) No, for some churches do not believe the very things that Jesus taught.

3 c) We should give God's Word to the world.

  9 a) By saying that He wanted His followers to be with Him wherever He was.

4 b) As God sent Jesus: to look for the lost and win them for the Lord.

Lesson 18: John 18

In this lesson you will study...
The Arrest of Jesus
Jesus Before Annas
Peter Denies Jesus
The High Priest Questions Jesus
Peter Denies Jesus Again
Jesus Before Pilate
Jesus Sentenced to Death

THE ARREST OF JESUS

Objective 1. *Explain how the arrest of Jesus shows that the forces of evil had no control over Him.*

Read John 18:1-11.

Judas led the soldiers to arrest Jesus. How could he do such a wicked thing? When a person turns away from Christ, he lets Satan have power over him.

Read verses 4 through 6 again. When Jesus said, "I am," the soldiers fell to the ground. They could not take Him prisoner unless He let them. But Jesus did not try to escape. He knew that it was God's plan for Him to die for our sins.

Jesus told the soldiers that those with Him should be allowed to go free for the soldiers were looking only for Him. Even as He was about to die, He thought of His own that they should not have to suffer as He would suffer.

Peter was ready to fight for his Lord. In fact, he drew out his sword and cut off the ear of a servant of the high priest. Luke tells that Jesus healed this man. Perhaps this was why Peter was not punished by the soldiers.

For You To Do

1 What lesson do we learn from Judas' betrayal of Jesus in the garden?
   a) We should not pray in a garden.
   b) We give Satan power over us when we turn away from Christ.
   c) Soldiers should not be allowed to attend prayer meetings.

2. Why did Jesus not run away or protect Himself when the soldiers came to arrest Him?
   a) He knew it was God's time for Him to die.
   b) He expected His disciples to protect Him.
   c) He had no power against soldiers.

3. What did Peter do in the garden?
   a) He prayed all night.
   b) He called down fire from heaven.
   c) He cut off the ear of the high priest's servant.

JESUS BEFORE ANNAS

Objective 2. *Explain how Peter's denial is instructive to believers.*

Read John 18:12-14.

Annas and his son-in-law Caiaphas had both held the office of high priest at different times. They had plotted together to kill Jesus. They were accusing Him of being a dangerous revolutionary leader. They said that if He were not put to death the Roman government would order their soldiers to kill all the people. Of course, this was not so. It was just the way that they could get the other religious leaders to ask the death sentence for Jesus.

Caiaphas had said that it was better for one man to die instead of all the people. He did not know that he was telling a great truth about Jesus' death. Jesus was the sacrifice for our sins so that we would not have to be punished.

You may wonder why Jesus could not save us without dying. God is good. He hates sin [dash] everything that is bad. So those who do wrong have to be separated from God. But since all life and happiness comes from God, those who are separated from Him have to die.

God taught us how awful sin is and how sin brings death by requiring a blood sacrifice before sins could be forgiven. Sheep, goats, and cattle were offered as sacrifices to take the place of the sinner.

According to the Law, almost everything is purified by blood; and sins are forgiven only if blood is poured out (Hebrews 9:22).

These animal sacrifices had to be repeated again and again because they could not take away sin. They were just a temporary arrangement until God sacrificed His own Son for us. Jesus would give His blood for us. If anything else could have saved us, God would never have let His only Son die for us.

For You To Do

4 Why did Jesus have to die to save us from our sins?
  - a) Because only by the shedding of His blood could our sins be forgiven completely.
  - b) Because we all have to die, and He died first to show us we need not fear death.
  - c) Because He wanted to teach that sacrifice for sin had to be repeated over and over again.

PETER DENIES JESUS

Read John 18:15-18.

The other disciple mentioned here was John, who wrote this gospel. He did not try to hide the fact that he was Jesus' disciple and he had no trouble. But Peter, who thought he would always be ready to speak up for Jesus, was afraid. He said he was not Jesus' disciple.

It is easy to let people know you are a Christian when you are with other Christians. It is not so easy when all the people around you are enemies of Jesus. What will you do?

If anyone declares publicly that he belongs to me, I will do the same for him before my Father in heaven. But if anyone rejects me publicly, I will reject him before my Father in heaven (Matthew 10:32-33).

For You To Do

5 Do you find it hard to let people know that you are a Christian?

No

Are you afraid they will persecute you?

No

Ask God to give you courage.

THE HIGH PRIEST QUESTIONS JESUS

Read John 18:19-24.

Annas had held the office of high priest, so he is called the high priest here, although Caiaphas held the position at this time. Annas tried to trap Jesus into saying something that they could use against Him in His trial, but Jesus would not answer his questions.

The soldiers took Jesus to Caiaphas' house. He was tried there by the religious court called the Sanhedrin. This trial was illegal. It was held secretly, at night, immediately after Jesus' arrest. There was no opportunity to call witnesses to speak in His defense. Most of the Sanhedrin had already decided that Jesus should be put to death. They just went through the form of a trial so that they could turn Him over to Pilate with an official accusation.

For You To Do

6 Why did Annas question Jesus?
   a) To learn His doctrine.
   b) To know more about Him.
   c) To try to trap Him.

PETER DENIES JESUS AGAIN

Read John 18:25-27.

Three times Peter was asked if he was not a follower of Jesus, and three times Peter denied his Lord. A rooster crowed, just as Jesus had said. When Jesus looked at him, Peter saw how he had failed his Master. He ran out crying, sorry for what he had done.

For You To Do

7 What did Peter do at the house of the high priest?
a) He cut off the ear of a servant of the high priest.
b) He denied his Lord three times.

JESUS BEFORE PILATE

Read John 18:28-38.

The Sanhedrin could not sentence anyone to death, so they sent Jesus to the Roman governor, Pilate. They accused Jesus of trying to set up His own kingdom. This was treason—a crime punishable by death.

Jesus did not try to defend Himself against this false accusation. He told Pilate that He was a king but

John 18 163

that His kingdom did not belong to this world. His kingdom is a spiritual kingdom in the lives of those who accept Him.

For You To Do

8 When Pilate asked if Jesus was a king, what did Jesus answer?
   a) "No, I have been falsely accused."
   b) "My kingdom does not belong to this world."
   c) "My kingdom is greater than the Roman Empire."

9 Have you accepted Jesus as king of your life?

Yes

JESUS SENTENCED TO DEATH

Read John 18:38-40.

In all the questioning, Pilate could not find any reason to condemn Jesus. He told the people this, but they shouted all the more for Jesus to be crucified. Pilate gave them a choice to allow Jesus or Barabbas, a robber, to be set free. The people chose Barabbas. People today are choosing sin and sinful pleasures over Jesus. What is your own choice? What will you do with Jesus?

For You To Do

10 What was Pilate's judgment?
 a) He said Jesus was guilty and should die.
 b) He said he found Jesus innocent.
 c) He would put Jesus in prison with Barabbas.

Check Your Answers

6 c) To try to trap Him.

1 b) We give Satan power over us when we turn away from Christ.

7 b) He denied his Lord three times.

2 a) He knew it was God's time for Him to die.

8 b) "My kingdom does not belong to this world.

3 c) He cut off the ear of the high priest's servant.

10 b) He said he found Jesus innocent.

4 a) Because only by the shedding of His blood could our sins be forgiven completely.

Lesson 19

John 19

In this lesson you will study...
Jesus Sentenced to Death
Jesus Nailed to the Cross
The Death of Jesus
Jesus' Side Pierced
The Burial of Jesus

JESUS SENTENCED TO DEATH

Objective 1. *Explain why Pilate sentences Jesus' to death.*

Read John 18:39-40; 19:1-16.

Pilate wanted to set Jesus free but he was afraid of the people. They were threatening to report him to the Roman emperor if he did not agree with them. His job and even his life would be in danger. He did not want to condemn an innocent person, but his own safety was more important to him than right or wrong. And so Pilate finally turned Jesus over to be nailed to a cross like a criminal.

Like Pilate, everyone who hears the good news about Jesus has to decide what to do with Him. Some are afraid to accept Jesus as Savior because of what other people will say or do. What God does with us on the judgment day depends on what we do now with His Son Jesus Christ.

For You To Do

1 Why did Pilate not free Jesus?
a) He found Jesus guilty.
b) He was afraid of the people.
c) He wanted to free Barabbas.

JESUS NAILED TO THE CROSS

Objective 2. *Explain the meaning and conflict of the Jesus' title that was placed on the cross.*

Read John 19:16-27.

Jesus was crucified, nailed to a cross between two criminals. A sign over him said: "Jesus of Nazareth, the King of the Jews." The chief priests did not like that, but Pilate refused to have it changed.

Even while Jesus was suffering on the cross, He thought of others rather than Himself. He gave His mother into the care of the disciple John. From other gospels we learn that He even prayed for God to forgive the people who had nailed Him to the cross.

For You To Do

2 What sign did Pilate have put on the cross where Jesus was crucified?
   a) Jesus of Nazareth who was guilty of treason.
   b) Jesus of Nazareth who broke the Law of Moses.
   c) Jesus of Nazareth, the King of the Jews.

THE DEATH OF JESUS

Read John 19:28-30.

All the Old Testament prophecies about the Messiah's death for our sins were fulfilled when Jesus died on the cross. It all happened just exactly like the prophets had predicted hundreds of years before, even to the soldiers gambling for His clothes and offering Him sour wine to drink.

In my thirst they gave me vinegar to drink (Psalm 69:21, KJV).

Jesus said: "It is finished!" He meant that He had finished the work that God had given Him to do. When He died, He finished paying for our salvation.

It was really our sins that made Jesus die. So we cannot put the blame on the people of Jesus' nation, or on Pilate, or on the soldiers who crucified Him. It was sin, our sin, that made Him go to the cross to save us. Knowing this makes us feel sorry for our sins. We do not want to keep on doing the things which caused Jesus' death. So we ask God to forgive our sins. We just accept what Jesus has done for us and we are saved. He died in our place.

> Christ himself carried our sins in his body to the cross, so that we might die to sin and live for righteousness (1 Peter 2:24).

For You To Do

3 What did Jesus mean when He said: "It is finished!"?
  a) A new world government was now in effect.
  b) The work of salvation was finished.
  c) All hope for His kingdom was lost.

4 Who is to blame for Jesus' death?
  a) Only the high priests.
  b) Just the Sanhedrin, Pilate, and the soldiers who crucified Him.
  c) We are, with everyone else who has sinned. Our sins made Him die.

5 What should we do now?
   a) We should never accuse anyone in court.
   b) We should blame the people who put Jesus to death and hold it against their descendants.
   c)) We should be sorry for our sins and ask God to forgive us.

JESUS' SIDE PIERCED

Objective 3. *Explain why it was important for Jesus' side to be pierced with a spear.*

Read John 19:31-37.

Crucifixion was a slow, agonizing form of execution. The soldiers broke the legs of the victims to make them die sooner. They found Jesus already dead and did not break His bones. This was a fulfillment of prophecy.

When the soldiers pierced Jesus' side, this also was the fulfillment of prophecy, the fountain opened to wash away our sins.

> In that day there shall be a fountain opened to the house of David and to the inhabitants of Jerusalem for sin and for uncleanness (Zechariah 13:1, KJV).

> The blood of Jesus, his Son, purifies us from every sin (1 John 1:7).

For You To Do

6 Memorize 1 John 1:7.

7 Read Zechariah 13:1 three times.

THE BURIAL OF JESUS

Read John 19:38-42.

Joseph of Arimathea and Nicodemus were both prominent religious leaders and members of the Sanhedrin. They had not voted for the death of Jesus. Up until now they had been secret believers in Jesus, afraid to come out openly for Him.

Sometimes it is hard for persons in a high social position to come out openly for Jesus. They may feel ashamed to go to a church where most of the people are poor. They may be afraid they will lose their jobs if they become Christians. But God gave Joseph and Nicodemus courage to ask for Jesus' body and to bury it, showing their respect and love for Him. This fulfilled another prophecy: that the Messiah would be with the rich in His death.

The burial custom there was to wrap the body with spices and place it in a cave or niche dug out of the rocky hillside. From the other gospels we learn that Jesus' body was buried in the tomb of Joseph of Arimathea.

There was not time to finish all the preparations for burial because it was nearly night when Jesus died. The Sabbath began at sundown. So the body of Jesus was put in the tomb without all the preparations for burial being finished.

For You To Do

8 What was done with Jesus' body?
   a) Joseph and Nicodemus buried it.
   b) The disciples buried it.
   c) It was left on the cross.

9 Why were the preparations for burial not finished?
   a) Jesus' followers were afraid.
   b) Jesus died just before the Sabbath began and no one could work after sundown.
   c) The disciples did not have enough money to buy the materials for burial.

10 Pray that God will give secret believers courage to come out openly for Jesus.

Check Your Answers

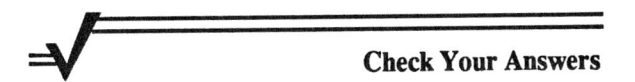

4 c) We are, with everyone else who has sinned. Our sins made Him die.

1 b) He was afraid of the people.

5 c) We should be sorry for our sins and ask God to forgive us.

2 c) Jesus of Nazareth, the King of the Jews.

8 a) Joseph and Nicodemus buried it.

3 b) The work of salvation was finished.

9 b) Jesus died just before the Sabbath began and no one could work after sundown.

Lesson 20: John 20

In this lesson you will study...
The Empty Tomb
Jesus Appears to Mary Magdalene
Jesus Appears to His Disciples
Jesus and Thomas
The Purpose of This Book

THE EMPTY TOMB

Objective 1. *Describe the two contrasting responses to the empty tomb.*

Read John 20:1-10.

Before Jesus was crucified He had told His disciples several times that He was going to be put to death. He let them know also that He would come back to life again. But when Jesus actually died, the disciples did not seem to remember what He had told them about His resurrection.

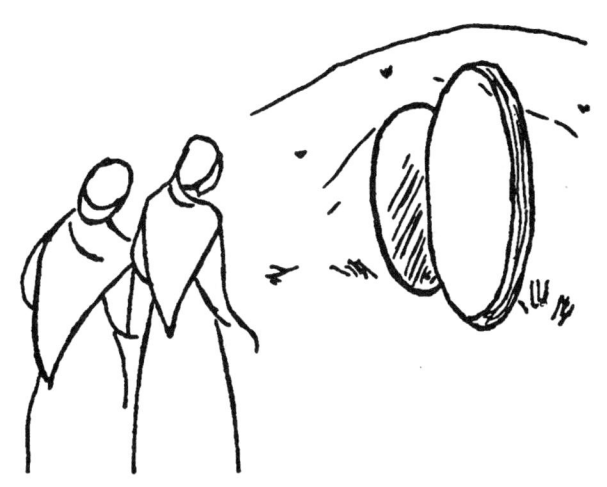

From the other gospel writers we learn that Mary Magdalene went with some other women to the grave where Jesus had been buried. They were going to put spices on the body, according to the custom. They saw that the great stone that had been put in front of the opening of the tomb had been taken away. The tomb was empty! Mary ran quickly to tell the disciples about it. While the other women stayed behind at the grave, an angel told them that Jesus was alive again.

Peter and John went to see for themselves. They found the tomb empty except for the cloths in which Jesus' body had been wrapped. Mary thought Jesus' enemies had stolen His body. But Peter and John knew that thieves would not take the time to unwrap the body and neatly roll the cloth which had been on Jesus' head. What had happened to Jesus? Thoughtfully they returned to the house where they were staying in Jerusalem.

For You To Do

1. Why did Mary Magdalene go to the tomb where Jesus was buried?
   a) She wanted to see if Jesus was really dead.
   b) She wanted to put spices on the body.
   c) She wanted to talk to the gardener.

2. What did she find when she reached the tomb?
   a) The tomb was open and empty.
   b) Joseph and Nicodemus were anointing the body.
   c) The enemies of Jesus had stolen His body.

3. What did Peter and John see when they went to the grave?
   a) They saw soldiers and asked what had happened.
   b) They saw the gardener and asked where Jesus' body was.
   c) They saw Jesus' grave-clothes in the empty tomb.

JESUS APPEARS TO MARY MAGDALENE

Objective 2. *Identify Jesus' various appearances following His resurrection.*

Read John 20:11-18.

Sometimes people are so sad over the death of a loved one that they cannot seem to believe the Word of

John 20

God. Even the message that the angels had given the other women at the tomb, the good news that Jesus was alive, had not convinced the disciples or Mary. They needed to meet Jesus personally to know that He really was alive.

Jesus comes to us too and lets us know that He is alive. He turns our tears to joy. And He sends us, like Mary Magdalene, to share the message with others. The women as well as the men have this responsibility. Mary was the first to see the risen Christ and to receive His message.

For You To Do

4 When Jesus came to Mary in the garden, what did He tell her?
a) To stop crying.
b) To go back home.
c) To go and give the disciples a message.

JESUS APPEARS TO HIS DISCIPLES

Read John 20:19-23.

That same day Jesus showed Himself to His disciples. They had locked themselves in a house, afraid that the enemies of Jesus would attack them next. When they saw Jesus, they could not believe that He really was alive again. Jesus showed them His hands and side and let them know that it was He and not a ghost. How happy they were when they knew that He was alive again!

Jesus said again that He was sending them just as the Father had sent Him. They would need special help for the work He was giving them, and He told them they would receive the Holy Spirit. We learn from the Gospel of Luke and the book of Acts that the disciples received the Holy Spirit about fifty days later on the Day of Pentecost. Jesus still gives the Holy Spirit to born-again Christians today who want to be used in His service.

The way the disciples obeyed Jesus' command would decide whether or not people would be saved. If they went out and preached the gospel, sinners would hear, repent of their sins, and be forgiven. But if the believers did not go with the gospel, sinners would never know the way of salvation. Their sins would not be forgiven because they would not know how to pray for forgiveness. When we are Christians, we should tell others about Jesus. If we know the resurrected Christ, and if we are filled with the Holy Spirit, we will surely be able to help others get saved.

For You To Do

5 What did Jesus tell the disciples?
  a) They should hide.
  b) He was sending them as the Father had sent Him.
  c) They should go home.

John 20

6 What special help did He promise them for the work He was giving them to do?
   a) He would pay them money to preach the gospel.
   b) He would give them joy; they would never have sorrow.
   c) He would give them the Holy Spirit.

7 In what way would they be able to save people from sin?
   a) By forgiving sins.
   b) By preaching the gospel.
   c) By burning candles.

JESUS AND THOMAS

Read John 20:24-29.

Thomas would not believe what the other disciples had seen. He doubted their experience and said he would have to see for himself.

Many people today think that Christians are deceived. They have to find out for themselves. If they are really sincere, they should pray: "Lord Jesus, if You are alive, come and let me know You." He will show Himself to them. Maybe their eyes will not see Him, but He will speak to their spirits. Then like Thomas they can say: "My Lord and my God!"

Jesus said to him, "Do you believe because you see me? How happy are those who believe without seeing me!" (John 20:29).

For You To Do

8 What did Thomas say when he saw Jesus?
a) "I do not believe it."
b) "You were right."
c) "My Lord and my God!"

THE PURPOSE OF THIS BOOK

Read John 20:30-31.

Of all the wonderful things that John had seen Jesus do and heard Him say, he wrote in his gospel those that would help us understand and know for sure that Jesus is the Son of God.

> These have been written in order that you may believe that Jesus is the Messiah, the Son of God, and that through your faith in Him you may have life (John 20:31).

For You To Do

9 Memorize John 20:31.

10 What is the purpose of John's gospel?
a) To let us know that Jesus is the Son of God.
b) To tell everything that Jesus did.

Check Your Answers

5 b) He was sending them as the Father had sent Him.

1 b) She wanted to put spices on the body.

  6 c) He would give them the Holy Spirit.

2 a) The tomb was open and empty.

  7 b) By preaching the gospel.

3 c) They saw Jesus' grave-clothes in the empty tomb.

  8 c) "My Lord and my God!"

4 c) To go and give the disciples a message.

  10 a) To let us know that Jesus is the Son of God.

Lesson 21

John 21

In this lesson you will study ...
Jesus Appears to Seven Disciples
Jesus and Peter
Jesus and the Other Disciple
Conclusion

JESUS APPEARS TO SEVEN DISCIPLES

Objective 1. *Explain the purposes of Jesus' appearing to the seven disciples at the Sea of Tiberias.*

Read John 21:1-14.

The disciples went back to Galilee where they had come from. They did not seem to know what Jesus wanted them to do. So, some of them went back to their old work of fishing.

The first time they went out to fish, they worked all night but did not catch anything. Jesus came and told them to put their nets down in the water on the other side of the boat. They did and caught so many fish that they could hardly pull the nets in. When we do what Jesus tells us to, He turns our failures into success.

For You To Do

1. What did the disciples do after Jesus had appeared to them?
   a) They went back to their homes in Galilee and went fishing. ✓
   b) They prayed to be filled with the Holy Spirit.
   c) They started preaching the gospel.

JESUS AND PETER

Objective 2. *Explain the purpose of Jesus' questions to Peter.*

Read John 21:15-19.

Peter had said three times that he did not know Jesus; now the Lord asked him a question three times. Peter had said that even though the others went away from Jesus, he would never leave Him. But he had acted worse than all the others when the test came. So Jesus asked him. "Do you love me more than these?" Peter was ashamed of the way he had acted and was sorry for what he had done.

Jesus said, "Feed my sheep." We understand from this that Peter was forgiven for denying the Lord. He was to be a shepherd to take care of those who would believe in Jesus. Again Jesus said to Peter, "Follow me."

For You To Do

2 What did Jesus ask Peter?
   a) "Do you love me more than these?"
   b) "Why did you deny me three times?"
   c) "Do you know how to take care of sheep?"

JESUS AND THE OTHER DISCIPLE

Read John 21:20-24.

John 21

John, who wrote this gospel, did not want to mention himself by name. He was the disciple that Peter was talking about when he asked: "Lord, what about this man?" Jesus let Peter know that it was not his business what John would have to do, or what would happen to him. Peter was to follow Jesus faithfully without worrying about what others would do.

God does not call all people to do the same thing. We cannot decide what we will do by what we see others doing. Neither can we say others should do a certain thing because we feel this is what God wants us to do. Let us pray for God's will in our own lives and in the lives of others Christians also.

For You To Do

3 What did Peter want to know?
  a) How he could feed sheep when he was a fisherman.
  b) What would happen to John.

4 Ask God to help you do His will.

CONCLUSION

Read John 21:25.

In the good news that John wrote, you have learned that Jesus is the Word. Through Him God speaks to you. Jesus is the Son of God who shows you what God is like. He is the Lamb of God who died to take away your sins.

Jesus is the way to heaven; follow Him and you will not be lost. He is the light of the world; you do not have to walk in darkness. Jesus is the bread of life who will satisfy your hungry soul. He is the truth who saves you from ignorance and error. He is the Son of Man who knows you and understands your needs. He is the Good Shepherd who cares for you. He is the resurrection and the life who gives you more abundant life now, victory over death, and eternal life in the world to come.

Jesus is all this and more. He is your Savior, Lord, and King who loves you. He wants you to love and obey Him. He wants you to follow Him now and be with Him forever in His heavenly home. Jesus will not force you to follow Him. He leaves the choice up to you. We hope that you follow Him faithfully and enjoy the wonderful life that He will give you.

We would like to help you learn more about Jesus so that you can follow Him better. The International Correspondence Institute has other courses that will help you grow spiritually. If you have not already sent for another course, do it today.

If you need help to find a good church near you, where you can meet with others who love Jesus, we will do what we can to help you find one. You will want to meet with others to pray, to worship God, and to study His Word. The pastor can help you with your spiritual problems. Do not forget to read the Bible and pray every day, and God will bless and keep you in His Love.

John 21

For You To Do

5 After studying who Jesus is and what He can do, what should you do now?
   a) Love Jesus—follow Him the rest of your life.
   b) Go your way—forget what you have studied.

6 Now you are reach to fill out the last half of your student report for Lessons 11-21. Review these lessons, then follow the instructions in your student report. When you send your answer sheets to your instructor, ask him about another course of study.

Check Your Answers

1 a) They went back to their homes in Galilee and went fishing.

   3 b) What would happen to John.

2 a) "Do you love me more than these?"

   5 a) Love Jesus—follow Him the rest of your life.

CONGRATULATIONS!

You have finished this course. We hope that it has been a great help to you! Remember to complete the second section of your student report and return the answer sheet to your instructor. As soon as we receive both answer sheets we will check them over and send you your certificate.

One Final Word

This is a special kind of book because it was written by people who care about you. These are happy people who have found good answers to many of the questions and problems which trouble almost everyone in the world. These happy people believe that God wants them to share with others the answers they have found. They believe that you need some important information in order to answer your own questions and problems and find the way of life that is best for you.

They have prepared this book in order to give you this information. You will find this book based on these fundamental truths:

1. You need a Savior. Read Romans 3:23, Exekiel 18:20.
2. You cannot save yourself. Read 1 Timothy 2:5, John 14:6.
3. God desires that the world should be saved. Read John 3:16-17.
4. God sent Jesus who gave his life to save all those who believe in Him. Read Galatians 4:4-5, 1 Peter 3:18.
5. The Bible shows us the way of salvation and teaches how to grow in the Christian life. Read John 15:5, John 10:10, 2 Peter 3:18.
6. You decide your eternal destiny. Read Luke 13:1-5, Matthew 10:32-33, John 3:35-36.

This book tells you how to decide your destiny, and it gives you opportunities to express your decision. Also, the book is different from others because it gives you a chance to contact people who prepared it. If you want to ask questions, or explain your needs and feelings, you may write to them.

In the back of the book you should find a card called *Decision Report and Request Card*. When you have made a decision, fill out the card and mail it as indicated. Then you will receive more help. You may use the card to ask questions, or make requests for prayer or information.

If there is no card in this copy of the book, write to your ICI instructor and you will receive a personal answer.

-----Clip and send to your ICI instructor.-----

CL2320 John's Gospel
Decision Report and Request Card

After studying this course, I have placed my trust in Jesus Christ as my Savior and Lord. I am returning this card with my signature and address to your ICI office for two reasons. First, to testify to my commitment to Christ and, second, to request information about more material to help me in my spiritual life.

NAME ....

ADDRESS ....

....

SIGNATURE ....

THE GREATEST OF ALL IS THE SERVANT OF ALL

Serving is an expression of love given to God for His consistent love. ICI courses are a vehicle of the Lord's that will assist you in developing into an effective and pleasing servant.

Using our courses will create an orderly system of Bible study and encourage a better understanding of spiritual truths.

To begin preparing for God's service we suggest enrolling in courses offered from our **Christian Service Program.**

Some courses from the **Christian Service Program** are:

CHRISTIAN MATURITY
THE KINGDOM, THE POWER AND THE GLORY
CORNERSTONES OF TRUTH
THE CHRISTIAN CHURCH IN MINISTRY
SPIRITUAL GIFTS
SOLVING LIFE'S PROBLEMS

If you desire a more detailed description about each course or directions on how to enroll in any of these courses contact your local ICI director.